ISAIAH

FORTRESS COMMENTARY ON THE BIBLE

Fortress Commentary on the Bible: The Old Testament and Apocrypha
Fortress Commentary on the Bible: The New Testament
The Pentateuch: Fortress Commentary on the Bible Study Edition
The Prophets: Fortress Commentary on the Bible Study Edition
Wisdom, Worship, and Poetry: Fortress Commentary on the Bible Study Edition
The Historical Writings: Fortress Commentary on the Bible Study Edition
The Gospels and Acts: Fortress Commentary on the Bible Study Edition
The Letters and Legacy of Paul: Fortress Commentary on the Bible Study Edition
Hebrews, the General Epistles, and Revelation: Fortress Commentary on the Bible Study Edition
1 and 2 Kings: Fortress Commentary on the Bible
Isaiah: Fortress Commentary on the Bible
Mark: Fortress Commentary on the Bible
1 and 2 Corinthians: Fortress Commentary on the Bible

ISAIAH

FORTRESS COMMENTARY ON THE BIBLE

MARVIN A. SWEENEY
CHRIS A. FRANKE

FORTRESS PRESS
Minneapolis

ISAIAH
Fortress Commentary on the Bible

31 30 29 28 27 26 25 1 2 3 4 5 6 7 8 9

Library of Congress Cataloging-in-Publication Data

Names: Sweeney, Marvin A. (Marvin Alan), author | Franke, Chris author
Title: Isaiah : Fortress commentary on the Bible / Marvin A. Sweeney, Chris A. Franke.
Description: Minneapolis : Fortress Press, [2026]
Identifiers: LCCN 2025035434 (print) | LCCN 2025035435 (ebook) | ISBN 9798341900110 paperback | ISBN 9798341900127 ebook
Subjects: LCSH: Bible. Isaiah--Commentaries
Classification: LCC BS1515.53 .S94 2026 (print) | LCC BS1515.53 (ebook)
LC record available at https://lccn.loc.gov/2025035434
LC ebook record available at https://lccn.loc.gov/2025035435

Cover design: Kris E. Miller
Cover image: compilation of stock textures from Getty Images

Print ISBN: 979-8-3419-0011-0
eBook ISBN: 979-8-3419-0012-7

CONTENTS

CONTRIBUTORS

Marvin A. Sweeney
Professor of Hebrew Bible
Claremont School of Theology

Chris A. Franke
Professor of Bible and Theology Emerita
St. Catherine University

Volume Editors

Gale A. Yee
Nancy W. King Professor of Biblical Studies
Episcopal Divinity School

Hugh R. Page Jr.
Associate Professor of Theology and Africana Studies
Vice President, Associate Provost, and Dean of the First Year of Studies
University of Notre Dame

Matthew J. M. Coomber
Assistant Professor of Biblical Studies
St. Ambrose University

ABBREVIATIONS

General

AT	Alpha Text (of the Greek text of Esther)
BOI	Book of Isaiah
Chr	Chronicler
DH	Deuteronomistic History
DI	Deutero-Isaiah
Dtr	Deuteronomist
Gk.	Greek
H	Holiness Code
Heb.	Hebrew
JPS	Jewish Publication Society
LXX	The Septuagint
LXX B	Vaticanus Text of the Septuagint
MP	Mode of production
MT	Masoretic Text
NIV	New International Version
NRSV	New Revised Standard Version
OAN	Oracles against Nations (in Jeremiah)
P.	papyrus/papyri
P	Priestly source
PE	Pastoral Epistles
RSV	Revised Standard Version
TI	Trito-Isaiah

Books of the Bible (NT, OT, Apocrypha)

Old Testament/Hebrew Bible

Gen.	Genesis
Exod.	Exodus
Lev.	Leviticus
Num.	Numbers
Deut.	Deuteronomy
Josh.	Joshua
Judg.	Judges
Ruth	Ruth
1 Sam.	1 Samuel
2 Sam.	2 Samuel
1 Kgs.	1 Kings
2 Kgs.	2 Kings
1 Chron.	1 Chronicles
2 Chron.	2 Chronicles
Ezra	Ezra
Neh.	Nehemiah
Esther	Esther
Job	Job
Ps. (Pss.)	Psalms
Prov.	Proverbs
Eccles.	Ecclesiastes
Song.	Song of Songs
Isa.	Isaiah
Jer.	Jeremiah
Lam.	Lamentations
Ezek.	Ezekiel
Dan.	Daniel
Hosea	Hosea
Joel	Joel
Amos	Amos
Obad.	Obadiah
Jon.	Jonah
Mic.	Micah
Nah.	Nahum
Hab.	Habakkuk
Zeph.	Zephaniah

Hag.	Haggai
Zech.	Zechariah
Mal.	Malachi

Apocrypha

Tob.	Tobit
Jth.	Judith
Gk. Esther	Greek Additions to Esther
Sir.	Sirach (Ecclesiasticus)
Bar.	Baruch
Let. Jer.	Letter of Jeremiah
Add Dan.	Additions to Daniel
Pr. Azar.	Prayer of Azariah
Sg. Three.	Song of the Three Young Men (or Three Jews)
Sus.	Susanna
Bel	Bel and the Dragon
1 Macc.	1 Maccabees
2 Macc.	2 Maccabees
1 Esd.	1 Esdras
Pr. of Man.	Prayer of Manasseh
2 Esd.	2 Esdras
Wis.	Wisdom of Solomon
3 Macc.	3 Maccabees
4 Macc.	4 Maccabees

New Testament

Matt.	Matthew
Mark	Mark
Luke	Luke
John	John
Acts	Acts of the Apostles
Rom.	Romans
1 Cor.	1 Corinthians
2 Cor.	2 Corinthians
Gal.	Galatians
Eph.	Ephesians
Phil.	Philippians
Col.	Colossians

1 Thess. 1 Thessalonians
2 Thess. 2 Thessalonians
1 Tim. 1 Timothy
2 Tim. 2 Timothy
Titus Titus
Philem. Philemon
Heb. Hebrews
James James
1 Pet. 1 Peter
2 Pet. 2 Peter
1 John 1 John
2 John 2 John
3 John 3 John
Jude Jude
Rev. Revelation (Apocalypse)

Journals, Series, Reference Works

ABD *Anchor Bible Dictionary*. Edited by David Noel Freedman. 6 vols. New York: Doubleday, 1992.
BibInt *Biblical Interpretation*
ConBOT Coniectanea biblica: Old Testament Series
JBL *Journal of Biblical Literature*
JNSL *Journal of Northwest Semitic Languages*
JSOT *Journal for the Study of the Old Testament*
JSOTSup Journal for the Study of the Old Testament Supplement Series
OTL Old Testament Library
SBLAIL Society of Biblical Literature Ancient Israel and Its Literature
SBLDS Society of Biblical Literature Dissertation Series
VT *Vetus Testamentum*
VTSup Supplements to Vetus Testamentum
ZAW *Zeitschrift für die alttestamentliche Wissenschaft*

Ancient Authors and Texts

Mishnah, Talmud, Targum

b. B. Bat. *Babylonian Talmudic tractate Baba Batra*

Isaiah 1–39

Marvin A. Sweeney

Introduction

ISAIAH 1–39 IS part of the larger sixty-six-chapter book of Isaiah, which is attributed to the prophet Isaiah ben Amoz, in Isa. 1:1. Isaiah was a Jerusalemite prophet who spoke during the reigns of the Judean kings Uzziah (783–742 BCE), Jotham (742–735), Ahaz (735–715), and Hezekiah (715–687/686).

The late eighth century BCE saw a number of events that had a major impact on the kingdoms of Israel and Judah. First was the Syro-Ephraimitic War in 735–732, in which Israel and Aram invaded Judah in an effort to force Judah to join their anti-Assyrian alliance. When King Ahaz of Judah appealed to Assyria for assistance, the Assyrian king Tiglath Pileser III destroyed Damascus, reduced Israel, and subjugated Judah. Second was the destruction of the northern kingdom of Israel by the Assyrians in 724–721, following its revolt against the Assyrian Empire. Third was Hezekiah's revolt against Assyria in 705–701, which saw the Assyrian king Sennacherib's invasion of Judah and siege of Jerusalem. Although the book of Isaiah claims a great victory for YHWH and Hezekiah, Assyrian records and archaeology confirm that Judah was devastated, although Jerusalem remained intact and Hezekiah remained on the throne.

Throughout this period, Isaiah advised against military confrontation with Assyria. Isaiah's theological worldview was heavily informed by the Davidic/Zion stream of ancient Judean thought, which posited an eternal covenant between YHWH, the royal house of David, and the city of Jerusalem. According to the Davidic/Zion tradition, YHWH would defend the house of David and the city of Jerusalem forever (see 2 Samuel 7). Isaiah therefore viewed political and military alliances between Judah and other nations as unnecessary and potentially dangerous. He consistently argued for reliance on YHWH as the best course for Judah's security.

Although the superscription attributes the book to the prophet Isaiah, interpreters since antiquity have recognized that major portions of the book were composed by other writers. Isaiah 40–66 appears to presuppose the conclusion of the Babylonian exile and the rise of King Cyrus of Persia in 539 BCE (see Isa. 44:28; 45:1), as well as later periods.

The Babylonian Talmud (c. 600 CE) attributes the book of Isaiah to King Hezekiah of Judah and his colleagues (*b. B. Bat.* 14b). The medieval commentator Rabbi Abraham Ibn Ezra (1089–1167 CE) hints at the possibility of a different author beginning in Isaiah 40. By the late eighteenth century, modern critical scholars recognized Isaiah 1–39 as a work based on the prophecies of Isaiah ben Amoz and Isaiah 40–66 as the work of later prophets from the exilic period and beyond. Bernhard Duhm's 1892 commentary first argued that the book of Isaiah presented the work of Isaiah ben Amoz in Isaiah 1–39, an anonymous prophet known as Deutero-Isaiah in Isaiah 40–55, and a third prophet known as Trito-Isaiah in Isaiah 56–66. Subsequent interpretation recognizes Trito-Isaiah as the work of multiple writers.

More recent scholarship focuses on reading the various components of the book of Isaiah as a literary whole. When Isaiah 1–39, 40–55, and 56–66 are read as a single work, they present the vision of Isaiah ben Amoz that spans some four to five hundred years of Judah's and Jerusalem's history and YHWH's activity in the world from the time of the Assyrian invasions in the late eighth century BCE through the anticipated recognition of YHWH as the sovereign ruler of all creation from the Jerusalem temple, the holy center for creation.

The process of the formation of the book over this period of time points to efforts in ancient Judaism to read Isaiah as a book that addresses later times as well. Second Isaiah and Trito-Isaiah both contain extensive intertextual citations of texts from Isaiah 1–39 that indicate reflection on the meaning of Isaiah's prophecies in relation to the end of the Babylonian exile and the early Persian or Second Temple period when the temple was rebuilt. Indeed, the final form of the book of Isaiah appears designed to persuade later generations of Jews that YHWH is indeed the true G-d of creation and that they should return to Jerusalem to acknowledge YHWH as the true sovereign of a restored Israel and Judah and the world at large.

The final form of the book of Isaiah is therefore designed to demonstrate YHWH's role as the true sovereign of creation and G-d of Israel/Judah. The first half of the book, in Isaiah 1–33, presents YHWH's plans to reveal worldwide sovereignty at Zion. These chapters argue that failure to recognize YHWH results in disaster, such as that realized by King Ahaz of Judah during the Assyrian invasions of Israel and Judah, whereas adherence to YHWH will result in security and restoration. The second half of the book, in Isaiah 34–66, argues that the time of restoration is at hand. Based on the model of King Hezekiah during the Assyrian siege of Jerusalem, the people need to turn to YHWH, who will return them to Jerusalem at the center of a restored creation.

The book of Isaiah is preserved in two major manuscripts from Qumran. The iconic 1QIsa^{a}, which dates to the late second century BCE, presupposes a proto-Masoretic text, although it includes many exegetical variations, including a clear division between Isaiah 33 and Isaiah 34 to mark the two halves of the book. 1QIsa^{b}, which dates to the first century BCE, preserves a proto-Masoretic text. Isaiah appears in some twenty-one other manuscripts from Qumran as well.

Jewish tradition reads the book of Isaiah as a book of comfort (*b. B. Bat.* 14b–15a) that anticipates the restoration of Jerusalem in the aftermath of disaster and exile. Selections from Isaiah are read throughout the year in the Jewish worship service as Haftarah readings, that is, readings from the Prophets that accompany the reading of the Torah portion at the center of the Jewish worship service. Many of the Haftarah readings from the ninth of Av, the Jewish day of mourning for the loss of the temple and other disasters, in the late summer through Rosh Hashanah, the Jewish Near Year, in the early fall, are drawn from Isaiah to anticipate divine restoration and blessing at the beginning of the New Year. According to Jewish tradition, Isaiah was put to death by

Hezekiah's evil son Manasseh, who sawed Isaiah in half after accusing him of being a false prophet (*b. Yev.* 49b; see also the pseudepigraphical work *The Martyrdom of Isaiah*).

Christianity also views the book of Isaiah as a key text in articulating Christian theology. Isaiah is quoted extensively throughout the New Testament, especially as a book that anticipates the coming of Christ. Indeed, Isaiah holds out a vision of an ideal world that Christianity understands to be realized through Jesus Christ. The reference to the birth of Immanuel in Isa. 7:14; the portrayal of the ideal king as the "Prince of Peace" in Isa. 9:1–6; and the Suffering Servant in Isa. 52:13–53:12 all play key roles in Isaiah's anticipation of Christ in the New Testament and Christian thought. The first part of Handel's *Messiah* (Dublin 1742) is based largely on texts from Isaiah.

Both Judaism and Christianity employ elements from Isaiah's commissioning vision in Isaiah 6, particularly the song of the Seraphim, "Holy, holy, holy, is the L-rd of Hosts, the whole earth is filled with [G-d's] glory" (6:3), as part of their respective worship services.

In the aftermath of the Shoah (Holocaust), both Jewish and Christian interpreters have begun to rethink the meaning of Isaiah. Isaiah's commission in Isaiah 6 to render the people blind, deaf, and dumb without the possibility of repentance, for instance, implies that G-d deliberately punishes innocent humans to reveal divine glory. Some maintain that Isaiah's commission calls not for acceptance of evil even when it comes from the highest authority, but instead for human beings to exercise moral responsibility in their own right to bring about the ideal world that Isaiah holds forth.

Isaiah 1

Prologue to the Book of Isaiah: YHWH's Intention to Purify Zion

The Text in Its Ancient Context

Isaiah 1 begins with the superscription for the book in 1:1. The superscription identifies the book as "the vision of Isaiah son of Amoz," and states that his focus is on Judah and Jerusalem. It places the prophet in the reigns of the Judean kings Uzziah (783–742 BCE), Jotham (742–735), Ahaz (735–715), and Hezekiah (715–687/668). Major events during this period include the Syro-Ephraimitic War (735–732), the fall of northern Israel to the Assyrian empire (722/1), and the Assyrian invasion of Judah and siege of Jerusalem (701).

Isaiah 1:2–20 constitutes the speech of the accuser in which the prophet lays out YHWH's charges that the people of Jerusalem, Judah, and Israel act like the people of Sodom and Gomorrah by not following divine guidance. Isaiah 1:21–31 constitutes the speech of the judge in which the prophet likens Jerusalem to unrefined ore that must be smelted to purge the city of its alleged sins. Once the process of punishment is complete, the prophet looks forward to Zion's restoration.

The Text in the Interpretive Tradition

Most modern scholars maintain that Isaiah 1 consists primarily of oracles by Isaiah son of Amoz, but it has been edited to serve as the prologue both to the book of Isaiah as a whole and to the first portion of the book in either Isaiah 1–39 or Isaiah 1–33 (Fohrer; Tomasino). It can function in this role because it presents an overview of the major concerns of the book, namely, YHWH's judgment against Jerusalem and Israel and the ultimate restoration of Jerusalem and Israel. Interpreters have noted its parallels with Isaiah 34, which opens the second half of the book of Isaiah, and Isaiah 66, which closes the book of Isaiah as a whole (Evans).

Christian tradition reads Isaiah 1 as a summary of the sins of Israel that calls for the coming of Jesus. Paul quotes Isa. 1:9 in Rom. 9:29 as part of his larger argument for justification by faith. Protestant Christian interpretation generally reads Isa. 1:10–17 as an indictment of temple ritual practice, although Jewish interpreters generally note that it condemns ritual practice that is not accompanied by proper moral and spiritual outlook (see Leviticus 19).

Jewish tradition reads Isa. 1:1–27 as the Haphtarah, or Prophetic Reading, for Shabbat Ḥazon, "the Shabbat of Vision," the first Shabbat after Tisha b'Av, "the ninth of Av," in late July or early August that commemorates the destruction of the First and Second Temples. The passage rehearses the theme of judgment that explains the destruction, but it points to restoration at the end.

The Text in Contemporary Discussion

Isaiah 1 is an indictment of human wrongdoing and rejection of G-d, but it looks forward to restoration once the people have been purged by divine punishment. In the aftermath of the Shoah or Holocaust, contemporary theologians recognize such statements as a form of theodicy, that is, they defend G-d against charges of divine wickedness, absence, and impotence by asserting that human beings—and not G-d—must be responsible for evil in the world.

Isaiah 2–4

YHWH's Plan for Worldwide Sovereignty at Zion

The Text in Its Ancient Context

Isaiah 2–4 begins with its own superscription in Isa. 2:1, which identifies the following material as "the word which Isaiah ben Amoz envisioned concerning Judah and Jerusalem" (author trans.). The unit presents the prophet's announcement concerning the preparation of Zion/Jerusalem for its role as the center for YHWH's worldwide sovereignty.

The Jerusalem temple was considered the holy center of creation. The portrayal of Jerusalem here as the site of the holy temple of YHWH, to which the nations would flock to learn divine instruction and bring an end to war, appears to presuppose the role that major temples played in Mesopotamian culture. During the Babylonian Akitu or New Year's festival, representatives of the nations subject to Babylonian rule would carry idols of their national gods in procession through the streets of Babylon to honor the Babylonian king. When the procession reached the temple of Marduk, the king would climb the steps to the top of the temple. There he would be granted the tablets of destiny, which gave him the right to rule the Babylonian Empire—and thus all creation—for another year on Marduk's behalf.

Following Isa. 2:2–4, the prophet presents three addresses that outline how the ideals expressed in this passage will be achieved. The first, in Isa. 2:5–9, begins with an invitation to the house of Jacob to join the nations' pilgrimage to Zion. But the passage quickly turns to accusations that the people have abandoned YHWH to follow foreign gods. As an adherent of the Davidic-Zion tradition, which maintains that YHWH alone protects the royal house of David and the city of Jerusalem, Isaiah opposed foreign alliances.

The second address, in Isa. 2:10–21, presents the prophet's announcement of the coming day of YHWH, when YHWH will punish foreign nations that threaten Israel (e.g., Isa. 13:6, 9; Joel 1:15; 2:11, 31; 3:14; Obad. 15) or those within Israel who allegedly oppose YHWH (e.g., Amos 5:18–20; Zeph. 1:7, 14; Mal. 4:5). The oracle focuses on the downfall of all who are high, mighty, and arrogant, and holds that YHWH alone will be aggrandized on the coming day of punishment.

The third address, in Isa. 2:22–4:6, focuses on the purging of Jerusalem and Judah. Following the plea in Isa. 2:22 to abandon human self-reliance, the passage turns to the punishment of the male leaders of Jerusalem and Judah in Isa. 3:1–11. The address then focuses on the leading women of Jerusalem and Judah in Isa. 3:12–4:1 who will be judged, stripped of their fine clothing, and left bereft of their husbands once the men have been killed or exiled. The passage concludes with an idyllic portrayal of a restored Jerusalem following the purge of the city.

The Text in the Interpretive Tradition

Many modern interpreters maintain that Isa. 2:2–4 (cf. Mic. 4:1–5) dates to the Babylonian exile in the sixth century BCE, because of the analogy with the Akitu festival and the passage's many affinities with Second Isaiah. Like Second Isaiah, the passage envisions peace among the nations who will recognize YHWH as the sovereign deity of all creation and the nations of the world. Isaiah 2–4 summarizes the message of the book of Isaiah as a whole, which envisions a process in which YHWH will bring punishment upon Jerusalem as a means to purge and restore the city, thereby to reveal YHWH's role as sovereign of all creation and the nations at large.

When read as part of the prophecies of Isaiah ben Amoz, the portrayal of judgment in Isaiah 2:5–4:6 functions as Isaiah's means to explain how the Assyrian Empire will be able to overrun Israel and Judah; namely, because the king and people do not place their faith in YHWH's promises of protection, YHWH brings the Assyrians to punish them for infidelity.

In both Jewish and Christian tradition, the passage is read as an eschatological portrayal of the future restoration of Jerusalem. The New Testament presupposes Isa. 2:2–4 in defining the imagery of the city on the hill in the salt and light parable of the Sermon on the Mount in Matt. 5:13–16. The city of light is a beacon to the good works of Jesus' followers and the glory of G-d in heaven. The reference to the city on a hill informs John Winthrop's 1630 sermon extolling the Massachusetts Bay Colonists to make their city (Boston) a shining example for the world.

Rabbinic commentators such as Abraham Ibn Ezra and David Kimḥi read the passage as a portrayal of the days to come when the temple would be rebuilt and the Messiah would come. The restoration of Zion is a key theme in both biblical and modern Zionist thought. Indeed, the BILU Zionist pioneers took their name from the first letters of the Hebrew words in Isa. 2:5, "O House of Jacob, come and let us go" (*bet ya'aqov, lekhu venelkhah*).

The Text in Contemporary Discussion

The idyllic imagery of Isa. 2:2–4, with its portrayal of the nations beating swords into plowshares and spears into pruning hooks, expresses one of the most important ideals of human life. Indeed, Isa. 2:4 serves as an unofficial motto for the United Nations. The English translation of the passage is inscribed on the Isaiah Stone, located in Ralph J. Bunche

Park just across the street from the United Nations headquarters in New York City.

But Isaiah 2–4 also employs images of divine judgment against all who are high, mighty, and arrogant. Although many read such accusations as justified indictments against sinful human beings, readers must remember that Isaiah was attempting to explain the realities—whether anticipated or realized—of foreign invasion in his own time. In the aftermath of the Shoah, or Holocaust, such attempts to explain evil by accusing the victims are coming increasingly under criticism. In the end, readers must remember that the prophets faced the same problems that contemporary thinkers face, namely, how to explain evil while simultaneously positing an omnipotent and moral G-d. Our own responsibility to establish an exemplary city on a hill becomes paramount.

Isaiah 5–12

Isaiah 5–12 is a lengthy unit that focuses on the Assyrian invasions of Israel and Judah and the restoration of Jerusalem and the Davidic monarchy once YHWH defeats the Assyrians. It includes two basic subunits, the prophet's announcement of judgment against Israel and Judah in Isaiah 5 and the prophet's explanation of the significance of divine judgment in Isaiah 6–12. Isaiah 6–12 includes three basic subunits, Isaiah's vision of YHWH in Isaiah 6; the account of YHWH's judgment against Judah during the Syro-Ephraimitic War in Isaiah 7:1–8:15; and the announcement concerning the fall of Assyria and the restoration of the Davidic kingdom in Isaiah 8:16–12:6.

Isaiah 5

Announcement of Judgment against Israel and Judah

The Text in Its Ancient Context

Isaiah 5 begins with the so-called vineyard allegory in Isa. 5:1–7, in which the prophet sings about his "friend's" unsuccessful efforts to grow good grapes in his vineyard. As the allegory progresses, it becomes evident that Isaiah's "friend" is indeed YHWH and that the vineyard with its sour grapes represents the people of Israel and Judah. A series of "woe" oracles then follows in Isa. 5:8–24, in which Isaiah, speaking on YHWH's behalf, charges the people with a series of crimes that illustrate their refusal to follow divine torah, "instruction" (5:24). The prophet's charges include illegal acquisition of land and houses (5:8–10), drunkenness and failure to heed the needs of the poor (5:9–17), impious demands for divine action (5:18–19), the confusion of good and evil (5:20–21), and the subversion of justice (5:22–23). YHWH's announcement of judgment, which portrays the approach of the Assyrian army, then concludes the subunit in Isa. 5:25–30.

The Text in the Interpretive Tradition

Modern interpreters maintain that Isaiah 5 is the product of Isaiah, but they note its intertextual relationships with the new song of the vineyard in Isa. 27:2–13, a sixth-century text, which looks forward to the restoration of Israel and Judah once the punishment is completed. The use of the "woe" oracle is particularly important because it warns of impending danger if the nation loses sight of its obligations for justice and righteousness in the world.

The Text in Contemporary Discussion

The approach of an enemy army is a terrifying prospect in both the ancient and the modern world. We in the United States have been blessed in that we have not suffered a foreign invasion since the War of 1812. Nevertheless, Isaiah's warning applies to us as well, insofar as he envisions leadership that is more interested in serving its own interests rather than those of the nation at large. Gridlock in the US Congress is a case in point, as our nation suffers from the inability of our Congressional representatives to arrive at compromises that will serve the larger good.

Isaiah 6

Isaiah's Commission Vision

The Text in Its Ancient Context

Isaiah 6 presents the prophet's autobiographical account of his vision of YHWH in the Jerusalem temple. Interpreters are divided as to whether this is a commissioning account or a later reflection concerning the prophet's failure to convince the people to repent. The issues include the placement of the chapter after Isaiah 1–5 rather than at the beginning of the book and YHWH's commission to render the people blind, deaf, and dumb so that they are unable to repent, which seems to contradict the prophet's efforts throughout the rest of Isaiah 1–39.

The account is an example of a throne vision in which YHWH appears to a human enthroned in the earthly or heavenly temple (1 Kings 22; Ezekiel 1; Daniel 7). The vision takes place in the year of King Uzziah's death (742 BCE), before the Syro-Ephraimitic War and the Assyrian invasions of the late eighth century. It is based on the imagery of the interior of the Jerusalem temple during worship. The prophet stands by the column at the entrance to the temple, where the king stands (2 Kgs. 11:14; 23:3) so that he can see into the interior of the temple (1 Kings 7). YHWH is enthroned over the ark of the covenant, which resides in the holy of holies of the temple. The portrayal of YHWH's train or robes billowing out of the temple is based on the imagery of smoke from the thick incense generated by the ten incense burners in the great hall of the temple. The portrayal of the seraphim (fiery angelic figures) is based on the imagery of the ten menorahs or candlestands, each with seven lamps, burning within the thick incense smoke. Their hymn, "Holy, holy, holy, is YHWH of Hosts, the whole earth is full of [G-d's] glory"(author trans.), represents the song of the Levitical choir during the temple liturgy. The rumbling noise is from the heavy doors that are opened at sunrise to inaugurate the daily morning worship service. The placement of a hot coal on

Isaiah's lips emulates the mouth-purification ceremonies practiced by Mesopotamian *baru* priests to prepare themselves to speak divine words. YHWH instructs Isaiah to render the people blind, deaf, and dumb so that they cannot repent and thereby save themselves. Isaiah does not object to YHWH's plans. Instead, he simply asks, "how long?" and YHWH responds with a vision of destruction (based on the Hebrew verb *sh'h*, which underlies the term Shoah) that will result in a surviving remnant of only 10 percent of the people. That remnant then constitutes "the holy seed" that will restore Jerusalem and Israel.

The Text in the Interpretive Tradition

Modern scholars have raised questions as to whether Isaiah 6 is the work of the prophet or not. Although some maintain that it is a later composition (e.g., Kaiser, 115–21) its portrayal of coming judgment in which the people are rendered blind, deaf, and dumb is a signal that it might represent the prophet's reflection on his inability to motivate the kings and people to change. Ezra 9:2 cites "the holy seed" from Isa. 6:13 as part of Ezra's portrayal of the restoration of Jerusalem in keeping with Isaiah's prophecies.

The New Testament cites Isa. 6:9–10 frequently. In Matt. 13:14; Mark 4:12; and Luke 8:10, the quote appears to validate the disciples of Jesus who understand his words. In John 12:39 and Acts 28:25, it appears as part of larger discussion concerning the failure of Jews to recognize Jesus as the Messiah. Although such comments were generated by early Christianity's attempt to argue for its own perspective, the condemnation of Jews would have repercussions throughout the Middle Ages and the modern period, culminating in the Shoah (Holocaust). The song of the Seraphim, "Holy, Holy, Holy . . ." constitutes part of the Trisagion (thrice holy) in Christian liturgy.

Judaism reads Isa. 6:1–13, together with Isa. 7:1–6 and 9:5–6, as part of the Haftarah for Exod. 18:1–20:26, which recounts the revelation of Torah at Sinai. The Haftarah aids in helping Jews to understand G-d as the sovereign monarch who stands behind the Sinai revelation.

The song of the Seraphim, "Holy, Holy, Holy . . ." constitutes part of the Kedushah (sanctification) of the morning and Musaf (additional) worship service in Judaism.

The Text in Contemporary Discussion

Mordecai Kaplan, the founder of Reconstructionist Judaism, finds a particularly disturbing issue is the moral character of YHWH's charge to the prophet to render the people blind, deaf, and dumb so that divine purpose might be realized (Kaplan). Such a position is an expression of teleological ethics, that is, the end result justifies the means. But the sacrifice of generations until that purpose is achieved hardly constitutes an example of ontological ethics, that is, the question of whether an act is good or evil in and of itself. Interpreters have noted that Isaiah does not challenge YHWH like Abraham (Genesis 18), Moses (Exodus 32; Numbers 14), Job, and others do when confronted with the possibility of divine evil. Ironically, Isaiah's ideal vision of world harmony among the nations (Isa. 2:2–4) is not realized and the book ends with the portrayal of the corpses of those who would resist YHWH (Isa. 66:24). Elie Wiesel (111) states that we can say anything to G-d from within Jewish tradition. The same applies to Christianity. Perhaps we should learn from this that Isaiah should have objected, just as we must object when confronted with evil even from the highest of authorities.

Isaiah 7:1–8:15

YHWH's Judgment against Judah

The Text in Its Ancient Context

Isaiah 7:1–8:15 presents an account of Isaiah's encounter with King Ahaz of Judah during the Syro-Ephraimitic War. Since the reign of King Jehu of Israel (842–815 BCE), the northern kingdom of Israel had been allied with the Assyrian Empire, which ensured that Israel would no longer be threatened by Aram as it was during the reigns of the Omride kings, that is, Omri (876–869 BCE), Ahab (869–850), Ahaziah (849), and Jehoram (849–842). But when King Pekah (737–732) came to the throne, he sought an alliance with Aram so that he might oppose the Assyrian Empire and bring an end to the crushing tribute that Israel had to pay. The Syro-Ephraimitic alliance therefore attempted to include all the small kingdoms of western Asia so they could present a united front against Assyria. King Jotham of Judah and his son Ahab refused to join the alliance. As Assyrian allies themselves, they knew that the Assyrians would devastate any kingdom that broke a treaty, and they likely distrusted an alliance based on two powers that had been at war with each other a century earlier. Consequently, northern Israel and Aram attacked Jerusalem in 734 BCE in an effort to force it into the Syro-Ephraimitic coalition.

The narrative portrays the fear of the house of David at the news of the Syro-Ephraimitic invasion of Judah. King Jotham apparently had passed away for reasons unknown to us, and his twenty-year-old son Ahaz was the new king. Ahaz was inspecting the water system of Jerusalem, located at the Upper Pool by the Fuller's Field ("fuller" means "one who does laundry"), which would have been located in the Kidron Valley east of Jerusalem outside the city's walls. The people of the city had access to the water through an underground tunnel, which represented a weak point in the city's defenses. Insofar as David had conquered Jerusalem by means of this tunnel (2 Sam. 5:8), Ahaz was considering how to defend the site. Isaiah's approach with his son, symbolically name Shear Jashub (Hebrew for "a remnant will return"), signaled the prophet's message that Ahaz should rely only on YHWH to defend the city, in keeping with YHWH's promise that the sons of David would sit on the throne of Israel in Jerusalem forever (2 Samuel 7). Of course, that would mean that many Judeans would die in keeping with the name of Isaiah's son, "(only) a remnant will return/survive." Ahaz preferred more practical means, however, and summoned the Assyrians to assist him as recounted in 2 Kings 16. Upon recognizing Ahaz's failure to trust in YHWH, Isaiah then proclaims that Judah will suffer as the Assyrians will invade and devastate the country, leaving

Judah to suffer under increased tribute. Although many believe Isaiah's advice to be impractical, it was based on the premise that the Assyrians would have invaded Aram and Israel anyway once their armies moved south to attack Jerusalem. The Assyrians destroyed Damascus and subjugated Israel, stripping it of its outlying territories. Pekah was assassinated. Ahaz's impetuousness did not result in an Assyrian reward; rather, it put him in Assyria's debt and resulted in heavier obligations to Assyria.

The Text in the Interpretive Tradition

Modern critics, particularly Peter Ackroyd, have noted that the Ahaz narrative in Isaiah 7:1–8:15 is formulated as a counterpoint to the presentation of Hezekiah in Isaiah 36–39. Ahaz appears to be unwilling to trust in YHWH or Isaiah, and Judah suffers invasion and subjugation to Assyria as a result. Hezekiah places his trust in YHWH and Isaiah in Isaiah 36–37, and the city of Jerusalem is delivered as a result. The two narratives thereby characterize their respective segments of the book. Isaiah 1–33 speaks especially of judgment like that experienced by Ahaz, whereas Isaiah 34–66 anticipates deliverance and restoration like that experienced by Hezekiah.

Matthew 1:23 cites the birth of Immanuel (Hebrew, "G-d is with us") in Isa. 7:14 as a prophecy that predicts the birth of Jesus. The Gospel, however, cites the Greek text of the Septuagint, which states that the boy will be born to a *parthenos*, "virgin," in keeping with Hellenistic tradition that celebrates children born to gods—for example, Zeus—and human virgins. The Hebrew text reads, *'almah*, "young woman," irrespective of her status as a virgin. Jewish interpreters understand Immanuel to be a son of Isaiah.

The Text in Contemporary Discussion

Just as Israel was invaded by Aram (Syria) and other nations, such as Egypt, Assyria, and Babylonia, in antiquity, so modern Israel has been invaded or attacked repeatedly by Syria, Egypt, Hezbollah, Hamas, and other Arab nations in modern times, for example, in 1948, 1967, 1973, 2006, and 2012. Israel stands at a geographical crossroads in the ancient and modern Middle East, and it is therefore a tempting target. Many see the Palestinian issue as the key issue of the Middle East, but the refusal by many Arab and Muslim countries to view Israel as a legitimate state for Jews is just as crucial.

Isaiah 8:16–12:6

Announcing the Fall of Assyria and Restoration of the House of David

The Text in Its Ancient Context

Isaiah 8:16–12:6 presents Isaiah's announcements concerning the fall of Assyria and the restoration of the Davidic kingdom. It includes two major components, namely, (1) prophetic instruction concerning YHWH's signs to Israel and the House of David in Isa. 8:16–9:6 (9:7 in NRSV) and (2) the prophet's announcement concerning the fulfillment of YHWH's signs in Isa. 9:7–12:6 (9:8–12:6 in NRSV).

Isaiah 8:16–9:6 begins with an expression of the prophet's frustration that Ahaz will not listen to him. He therefore announces his intention to "bind up the testimony and seal my instruction [torah] among my teachings" while he waits for YHWH, who is hiding the divine face from the house of Israel. He envisions the people walking in great darkness until such time as a new and righteous Davidic monarch will emerge who will be recognized as "the prince of peace."

Isaiah 9:7–12:6 announces the fulfillment of YHWH's signs. The passage begins with a lengthy sequence of oracles, all based on the formula "YHWH's hand is stretched out still," which condemn the northern kingdom of Israel in Isa. 9:7–10:4 for a variety of misdeeds. This oracular sequence constitutes the prophet's comment on the fall of the northern kingdom of Israel to the Assyrian empire in 722/721 BCE. With Israel destroyed, Isaiah then turns in Isa. 10:5–12:6 to a condemnation of the Assyrian Empire, particularly its king (presumably Sargon II), for his arrogance in threatening Jerusalem and claiming to be the true power in the world. In Isa. 10:5–34, Isaiah likens the Assyrian king to the Egyptian Pharaoh of the exodus, when he announces that the Assyrian king will fall just like a tree that has been trimmed. YHWH will grow a new, righteous Davidic monarch from the stump of Jesse. The prophet holds in Isa. 11:1–16 that the new monarch will be wise and righteous, that he will reunite Israel and Judah, and that he will swoop down on the enemies of Israel and Judah, resulting ultimately in the return of exiles from Assyria and Egypt. The concluding hymn in Isa. 12:6 draws its language from the Song of the Sea in Exodus 15, especially in verses 1–3, and various Psalms, such as 105:1 and 118:14, 21, to praise YHWH for restoring Israel and Judah.

The Text in the Interpretive Tradition

Modern interpreters debate compositional issues in Isaiah 8:16–12:6. Although many view the royal oracle in Isa. 9:1–6 as Isaiah's anticipation of the birth of Hezekiah, they see the royal oracle of Isa. 11:1–16 as a postexilic composition. Isaiah 11 was more likely written in the time of King Josiah of Judah (640–609 BCE), who was known for his program of religious reform and national restoration. The reign of Josiah saw many editions of the narrative and prophetic books, such as Joshua–Kings, Isaiah, Amos, Hosea, and portions of Jeremiah that were edited to support the Josian reform. Isaiah 11, with its vision of a child king who would reunite Israel and Judah to bring home the exiles from Assyria and Egypt, is an example of such work. The hymn in Isa. 12:1–6 points to a liturgical setting for the performance of Isaiah, perhaps in the monarchic period as well as in the second temple of the Persian period and beyond.

Isaiah's royal oracles have been a source of constant attention in Christianity insofar as they are read as predictions of the coming of Jesus. The reference in Isaiah 8:23–9:1 (9:1–2 in NRSV) to the people who have seen a great light appears in Matt 4:15–16 as part of the evangelist's introduction to Jesus' career in the Galilee. Likewise, the phrase "a child is born" in Isa. 9:6 stands in the background of the birth of Jesus in Matt. 1:23. Isaiah 9:1–6 plays a key role in Handel's oratorio *The Messiah* (Dublin 1742), which is performed especially at Christmastime to celebrate Jesus' birth and life. Paul cites Isa. 11:1, 10, in Rom. 15:12 as part of a larger argument that the new Davidic king is a sign to the nations.

Talmudic tradition views Isa. 9:1–6 as a reference to the birth of Hezekiah. The talmudic Rabbi Bar Ḳappara thought that Hezekiah was supposed to be the Messiah, but the attribute of justice (*middat ha-din*) argued against this claiming that David was not made the Messiah and that Hezekiah was less worthy (*b. Sanh.* 94a). Isaiah 10:32–12:6 functions as the Haftarah reading for the eighth day of Passover because of its exodus references, its portrayal of the downfall of an oppressive king, and its vision of exiles restored to Israel and Judah from Egypt and Assyria.

The Text in Contemporary Discussion

The celebration of the downfall of an oppressor expresses an important ideal in both Christianity and Judaism. In Christianity, such ideals are expressed through the coming of Christ, who brings down the oppressive powers of the world. In Judaism, such ideals are expressed especially in the celebration of Passover and the release of the people of Israel from Egyptian bondage. We may also remember the joyous celebrations at the end of World War II, when both Nazi Germany and imperial Japan surrendered. The famed picture of the sailor kissing the nurse in Times Square is a lasting reminder of the joy experienced as a result of the end of the war. At the same time, we must remember the limits of military power. The killing of Osama bin Laden, however satisfying given his crimes, did not bring the war on terrorism to an end.

Isaiah 13–27

Isaiah 13–27, concerned with the preparation of the nations for YHWH's worldwide sovereignty, constitutes a distinctive section within the book of Isaiah as a whole. It contains two basic components. The first is the announcement concerning the nations in Isaiah 13–23, including Babylon (Isaiah 13–14), Moab (Isaiah 15–16), Damascus (Isaiah 17–18), Egypt (Isaiah 19–20), the Wilderness of the Sea (Isa. 21:1–10), Dumah (Isa. 21:11–12), Arabia (Isa. 21:13–17), the Valley of Vision (Isaiah 22), and Tyre (Isaiah 23). The second concerns the restoration of Zion/Israel at the center of the nations. All of the nations mentioned were part of the Persian Empire, which indicates that the book of Isaiah associates YHWH with Persian rule.

Isaiah 13–14

The Pronouncement concerning Babylon

The Text in Its Ancient Context

Like all of the oracles against the nations in Isaiah 13–23, Isaiah 13–14 begins with a superscription that labels the following text as the *massa'*, or "pronouncement," concerning Babylon. The prophetic pronouncement functions as a means to depict YHWH's actions in the world.

Isaiah 13–14 is a lengthy oracle that anticipates the downfall of Babylon on the day of YHWH. The day of YHWH tradition is well known in the Prophets as a day when YHWH will act against enemies, including those who threaten Jerusalem, Judah, and Israel (e.g., Joel 1–2; Obadiah; Zeph. 1:2–18), and even against Jerusalem or Israel itself when viewed as acting contrary to YHWH's expectations (e.g., Isa. 2:6–21; Amos 5:18–20). King Hezekiah of Judah allied with the Babylonian prince Merodach Baladan in his attempt to revolt against the Assyrians in 705–701 BCE. The aim of the revolt was to strike Assyria from both west (Judah and its allies) and east (Babylon and its allies) and thereby divide Assyrian efforts to put down the revolt. Isaiah's opposition to this alliance is evident in Isaiah 39, where Isaiah condemns Hezekiah for receiving the Babylonian embassy in preparation for the revolt.

A short oracle against the Philistines is appended in Isa. 14:28–32 to account for one of the nations subdued by Hezekiah as he prepared for revolt.

The Text in the Interpretive Tradition

Most scholars recognize that Isaiah 13–14 is the product of later editing, particularly in the sixth century BCE, when the Persians conquered the Babylonian Empire and allowed exiled Jews to return to Jerusalem to rebuild the temple. Isaiah 13 in particular appears to have been composed to anticipate the work of Second Isaiah in Isaiah 40–55, which announced the end of the exile and called on Jews to return to Jerusalem. The passage appears to have reworked an older anti-Assyrian oracle in Isaiah 14 that celebrated the battlefield death of the Assyrian monarch Sargon II in 705 BCE. His defeat was so complete that his body laid unrecovered and unburied on the battlefield (see Isa. 14:19–20). Sargon's death was an important catalyst for Hezekiah's revolt in 705 BCE. The brief anti-Assyrian oracle in Isa. 14:24–27 points to the original Assyrian referent of the oracle and demonstrates how earlier Isaian prophecies could be reread in reference to later events following the lifetime of the prophet.

Interpreters have long noted the portrayal in Isa. 14:12 of the fall of Helel son of Shachar, "the Shining One, son of the Dawn," from heaven down to Sheol (the netherworld where all of the dead go; see esp. Erlandsson). Although this was originally meant as a reference to Sargon II, later interpreters viewed it as a description of a fallen angel from heaven who would then become the Satan figure. Thus the Vulgate translates the phrase into Latin as Lucifer, "light bearing" (in reference to the morning star, Venus), which became a name for Satan in the Christian tradition. Although the downfall of Lucifer comes to play a role in Christian eschatology, early Protestant interpreters such as Luther and Calvin denied that this text referred to Satan, preferring instead to see it as a historical reference to Babylon. Jewish interpreters tended to read the name in relation to the Babylonians. Rashi saw it as a reference to Venus, the morning star, which symbolized the Babylonian goddess Ishtar, and Kimḥi understood it as a reference to Nebuchadnezzar.

The Text in Contemporary Discussion

Many interpreters read Isaiah 13–14 as an oracle proclaiming the downfall of Iraq during the 1991 Gulf War, especially when Saddam Hussein parked Iraqi fighter jets by the ruins of Ur, located in the territory of ancient Babylonia, in an attempt to protect them from allied forces. Saddam Hussein attacked Israel with Scud missiles in an attempt to draw Israel into the war and thereby prompt Arab allies of the United States such as Egypt and Syria to reconsider their participation in the US-led alliance. Iraq's Scud missiles lacked precision guidance systems, and they generally struck civilian rather than military targets. Israel was not an active member of the alliance—indeed, the United States, in an effort to attract Arab nations into the alliance, had advised Israel to stay out of the war altogether. Nevertheless, Saddam Hussein hoped to draw on the anti-Jewish sentiments of America's Arab allies by deliberately attacking Israel despite the fact that it was not directly involved.

Others see environmental concerns addressed in this text, particularly in Isa. 14:7–8 in which the trees celebrate the downfall of the King Babylon because he would no longer come to cut them down (Tucker, 161). Mesopotamian rulers were known for their expeditions to Phoenicia (modern Lebanon) to cut down cedars and other trees to decorate their imperial palaces.

Isaiah 15–16

The Pronouncement concerning Moab

The Text in Its Ancient Context

Isaiah 15–16 is Isaiah's oracle concerning Moab, located east of the Jordan River and Dead Sea in modern-day Jordan. The oracle describes Moab's distress at a foreign invasion, likely the Assyrian king Tiglath Pileser III, during the Syro-Ephraimitic War (734–732 BCE). The city names indicate a flight from the region north of the Wadi Arnon, which would have been Israelite territory settled by Reuben and Gad prior to the ninth-century-BCE war between Aram and Israel. Seeing Israel's defeat by Aram, King Mesha of Moab seized Israelite territory north of the Arnon, as recorded in his famed Moabite Stone. In Isa. 16:6, the prophet recalls Moab's arrogance.

The Text in the Interpretive Tradition

Although this text was likely written by Isaiah, it was reused in later contexts. It likely provided support for Josiah's interests in reestablishing Davidic rule over Moab in the late seventh century BCE. Portions of the oracle were reused in Jeremiah's oracle concerning Moab in Jer. 48:29–38.

The Text in Contemporary Discussion

Isaiah 16:3–5 is frequently cited in support of causes for social justice. Gene M. Tucker, for example, understands this section to be a reference to refugees from war. He states, "The visionary poet sees the answer to the problems of refugees from war to be in a ruler descended from David, on the throne in Jerusalem. The passage is messianic in this hope for an anointed one in the future. Its vision of a time of peace under a just ruler reiterates the themes of 11:1–5" (Tucker, 169).

Isaiah 17–18

The Pronouncement concerning Damascus

The Text in Its Ancient Context

Isaiah 17–18 constitutes the prophet's pronouncement against Damascus, the capital of Aram (Syria), but the reference to Ephraim and Israel in Isa. 17:3 indicates that it addresses the Syro-Ephraimitic coalition that threatened Jerusalem and Judah in 734–732 BCE. The woe oracle against Cush (Ethiopia) in Isaiah 18 presupposes King Hosea of Israel's embassy to Cush in 724 BCE, in preparation for its ultimately fatal revolt against Assyria. Isaiah is opposed to such alliances, as they indicate a failure to put trust in YHWH.

The Text in the Interpretive Tradition

The Aramaic *Targum Jonathan* reads the reference to Cush in Isa. 18:1 as India, which prompted medieval Jewish interpreters such as Rashi and Kimḥi to read Isaiah 18 as a depiction of the eschatological war against Gog of Magog (Ezekiel 38–39).

The Text in Contemporary Discussion

The prophet's condemnation of Damascus raises the issue of judgment against the Assad regime of modern Syria, which is also creating for itself a heap of ruins. Hafez al-Assad was a member of the minority Alawite sect of Shia Islam who served as air force commander under the leadership of the Baathist party. He came to power by instigating two internal military coups in 1969 and 1970 to oust the leadership of his own Baathist party. Under his rule as president of Syria, Hafez al-Assad (1971–2000) was known for its belligerency against Israel, particularly the Yom Kippur War of 1973, and its suppression of dissent, particularly the killing of some twenty thousand Muslim Brotherhood supporters in Hama in 1982. Although many saw his son, Bashar al-Assad (2000–present) as a potential reformer, the outbreak of the Syrian civil war, which has now seen over one hundred thousand killed, has dashed any such hopes. Many are concerned about the future of Syria, insofar as the Syrian rebels are heavily influenced by al-Qaeda and other Islamic extremists. Assad himself is supported by Hezbollah soldiers, who are allies of Iran.

In both Isaiah 17–18 and in this modern example, we find some of the fatal consequences that come with the lust for, and desire to cling to, power. Assad's desperation to hold on to power has led to the use of chemical weapons against his own people. In one attack on August 21,

2013, over 1,400 Syrian civilians, including women and children, were killed in a gas attack apparently launched by the Syrian army. The Assad regime has responded by claiming that the attack was carried out by the Syrian rebels, but the rebels lack access to such weapons and the means to deliver them. This desperate move has now led Assad's allies to join with a United Nations resolution to strip him of his chemical arsenal, and may ultimately lead to his undoing.

Isaiah 19–20

The Pronouncement against Egypt

The Text in Its Ancient Context

Isaiah's pronouncements against Egypt in Isaiah 19–20 presuppose the role that Egypt played in the late eighth century in instigating revolt against the Assyrian Empire. Isaiah was opposed to military alliances between Judah and foreign powers. He points to internal struggle within Egypt during the late eighth century that eventually brought the Egyptian twenty-fifth (Ethiopian) dynasty to power as a sign of Egyptian instability. Isaiah 19:16–25 may presuppose the Assyrian conquest of Egypt in 671 and the subsequent rise of the twenty-sixth (Saite) dynasty as an Assyrian ally. Isaiah's walking about Jerusalem naked and barefoot in Isaiah 20 following the conquest of Ashdod by Sargon II in 715 BCE is a prophetic symbolic action meant to demonstrate the fate of those who would support an Egyptian and Ethiopian-inspired revolt against Assyria.

The Text in the Interpretive Tradition

Egypt ultimately became a major center for Jewish life in antiquity, prompted initially by the movement of refugees from the eighth-century Assyrian invasions and subsequent political and trade relations in the Persian, Hellenistic, and Roman periods. Although Egypt was the birthplace of the Greek Septuagint in the Hellenistic period, the emergence of antisemitism in the Roman period placed the Egyptian Jewish community at risk (see Schäfer).

The Text in Contemporary Discussion

Although Egypt was the site of an important Jewish community from antiquity through the medieval and early modern periods, the Egyptian government expelled the bulk of its Jewish community and seized its property in the aftermath of the creation of modern Israel in 1948. President Anwar Sadat of Egypt signed a treaty with Israel in 1979 that saw the return of the Sinai to Egyptian control, but Sadat was assassinated in 1981 for his initiative and the treaty has remained rather cold to this day. The ongoing political and religious struggles between factions raise great concerns for the future of the treaty and for the Christian community in Egypt.

Isaiah 21

Pronouncements concerning the Wilderness of the Sea, Dumah, and Arabia

The Text in Its Ancient Context

Isaiah 21 is not a single text, but it is a sequence of prophetic pronouncements concerning the Wilderness of the Sea in Isa. 21:1–10; Dumah in Isa. 21:11–12; and Arabia in Isa. 21:13–17. The reference to Babylon's fall in 21:9 indicates that the Wilderness of the Sea refers to Babylon. The term refers to the marshy area where the Tigris and Euphrates join and flow out into the Persian Gulf, that is, the modern Shatt al-Arab Waterway. Hezekiah's Babylonian ally in his revolt against Assyria (see Isaiah 39), Prince Merodach Baladan, used the area as a base to hide from the Assyrians and to conduct guerrilla operations against them. Dumah is the name of an Arabian Desert oasis conquered by the Assyrian king Sennacherib in 689. It is associated with Seir, another name for Edom. The Assyrians conducted campaigns against the

Arabian tribes in the late eighth and seventh centuries. The present oracle presupposes Sennacherib's defeat at Kedar in the northern Arabian Desert in 689.

The Text in the Interpretive Tradition

A. A. MacIntosh points to the reference to Elam and Media in Isa. 21:2 as an indication that Isaiah 21 is a palimpsest, that is, a text that has been rewritten in relation to later circumstances. Babylon fell to a combination of Elamites and Medes in 539 BCE under the leadership of Cyrus. It appears that the concern with the anticipated downfall of Merodach Baladan has been updated to account for Babylon's fall to Cyrus.

Isaiah 21:9 is cited in Rev. 18:2 as part of the scenario concerning the fall of Babylon (Rome).

The Text in Contemporary Discussion

The reference to the watchtower in Isa. 21:8–9 inspired the title of *Watch Tower*, the publication of the Jehovah's Witnesses. The Jehovah's Witnesses believe that the destruction of the present world order through Armageddon is imminent and that the kingdom of G-d is at hand. The image of the watchtower in Isa. 21:8–9 therefore symbolizes their watchfulness in preparing for the advent of G-d's kingdom. The downfall of Babylon was symbolic of the eschatological age in Christianity when Christ would be revealed to all (Revelation 18–19).

Isaiah 22

The Pronouncement concerning the Valley of Vision

The Text in Its Ancient Context

Isaiah 22 is called the pronouncement concerning the Valley of Vision, but the contents of the oracle make it clear that it refers to Jerusalem after the lifting of Sennacherib's siege in 701 BCE. Although Isaiah 36–37 claims a great victory over Sennacherib, his records indicate that Hezekiah saved the city and his throne by capitulating to the Assyrians. Isaiah points out the cost of the siege, namely, Jerusalem was spared but the land of Judah was devastated.

Isaiah refers to Hezekiah's water tunnel, built in preparation for the revolt. He condemns Shebna, a major government official under Hezekiah, for building his own tomb at a time of national threat. An ancient inscription marking the tomb of Shebna has been discovered in the Kidron Valley east of biblical Jerusalem in the Arab Silwan village.

The Text in the Interpretive Tradition

Isaiah 22:13, "let us eat and drink, for tomorrow we will die," appears in 1 Cor. 15:32 to characterize Paul's opponents who do not believe in Jesus' resurrection. The reference to the key of the house of David in Isa. 22:22 appears in Rev. 3:7 to indicate to the church in Philadelphia that the door (to Christ) is open to them.

Talmudic tradition holds that Shebna was the high priest who shot an arrow to the Assyrians with the message that all Jerusalem—except Hezekiah and Isaiah—were ready to surrender (*b. Sanh.* 26ab; see also Rashi).

The Text in Contemporary Discussion

Premature celebrations of victory often mask reality. Japan celebrated a premature victory over the United States at Pearl Harbor in 1941 without realizing that they had planted the seeds of their own national destruction. Likewise, although the United States was able to claim victory in Iraq, it now has little influence in Iraq. From politicians who claim victory too early to office workers who Twitter about promotions before they have been secured, this text serves as a valuable warning against the sorts of hubris that lead people to snatch defeat out of the jaws of victory.

Isaiah 23

The Pronouncement against Tyre

The Text in Its Ancient Context

Isaiah's pronouncement concerning Tyre targets one of Hezekiah's principal allies in his revolt against the Assyrians. Tyre was the dominant Phoenician city, and it was the major sea power of the day, with a powerful navy and extensive trade relations. But when Sennacherib unexpectedly subdued the island city in 701 BCE, Hezekiah's western allies quickly abandoned him, leaving him to face the Assyrians alone.

The Text in the Interpretive Tradition

The oracle has been updated in Isa. 23:13–18 to account for Tyre's fall to the Babylonians in 588–572 BCE. Like Jerusalem, the oracle anticipates that Tyre will rise again in seventy years (cf. Jer. 25:29 on Jerusalem).

The Text in Contemporary Discussion

The issue of being abandoned by one's allies that is raised in Isaiah 23 is still applicable in a plethora of modern contexts, whether it be betrayal on an international scale or within the family relationships. Modern Lebanon fell victim to its internal divisions between its Maronite Christian, Druze, and Muslim populations. The Palestine Liberation Organization (PLO) moved into Lebanon following its failed attempt to take over Jordan in 1971, and thereby played an important role in destabilizing the country. The Lebanese civil war of 1975–1990 saw the disintegration of Lebanon as a coherent modern state. Israel invaded Lebanon in 1982 to counteract the PLO, and later withdrew in 2000 following its failure to establish Maronite Christian control of the country. Lebanon is now dominated by Hezbollah (Party of G-d), a heavily armed Shiite Muslim militant military organization and political party backed by Iran. Lebanon never signed a peace treaty with Israel following the 1948 war of independence. Hezbollah attacked

Israel from southern Lebanon in 2006, raining missiles on Haifa and other parts of the country, and Israel counterattacked with air, naval, and ground units. In the aftermath of the conflict, both the Lebanese government and the United Nations abandoned their commitments to disarm Hezbollah, leaving Israel to feel abandoned by a major governing body to which it belongs.

Isaiah 24–27

YHWH's New World Order: Salvation for Zion/Israel

The Text in Its Ancient Context

Isaiah 24–27 concludes the oracles concerning the nations in Isaiah 13–27 with an extensive prophetic announcement concerning YHWH's new world order based in Zion. This section envisions a future withering of creation and judgment against the earth in Isa. 24:1–23 followed by a prophetic announcement of YHWH's blessing in Isaiah 25:1–27:13. This latter section includes YHWH's blessing of the earth at Zion in Isa. 25:1–12 and its results in Isa. 26:1–27:13, including an account of Judah's petition to YHWH for deliverance in Isa. 26:1–21; YHWH's defeat of Leviathan in Isa. 27:1; and an exhortation to Israel to accept YHWH's offer of reconciliation.

Isaiah 24:1–23 presents the prophet's announcement of YHWH's punishment of the earth. The portrayal of a devastated and withered land is a typical element of blessings and curses speeches, for example, Leviticus 26 and Deuteronomy 28–30, that posit natural catastrophe as a consequence of human failure to abide by the divine will. The prophets employ them constantly for the same purpose (e.g., Isa. 34:11–17; Jer. 5:6; 19:7–9; Hosea 4; 13:7–8). The imagery presupposes the period of the late summer prior to the onset of the fall rains and the New Year that inaugurates the restoration of divine rule over the world of creation. In the present instance, the withered earth presages the fall of the "city of chaos" (Isa. 24:10), that is, Babylon, and the recognition of YHWH's reign.

Isaiah 25:1–12 inaugurates the announcement of blessing with a portrayal YHWH's blessings for Zion. The imagery includes a banquet for the nations at Mt. Zion in which death will be banished forever. Such a banquet is based on the celebration of the fall festival of Sukkot, "Booths," which celebrates the completion of the summer harvest and anticipates the onset of the fall rains. In Mesopotamian cultures, the fall rains were celebrated as the time when fertility gods, such as Tammuz, were returned to life from the netherworld.

Isaiah 26:1–21 presents Judah's petition to YHWH for deliverance. The liturgical dimensions of the passage emerge here insofar as it employs an initial hymn of praise in 26:1b–6 to celebrate YHWH's deliverance of the land from the wicked city of chaos. The imagery of childbirth in 26:17–18 complements the imagery of resurrection of the dead in 26:14 and 19 to give expression to YHWH's life-giving deliverance of the people.

Isaiah 27:1 presents a brief reference to YHWH's defeat of Leviathan, the seven-headed chaos monster of the deep known also in Ugaritic/Canaanite mythology (see also Ps. 74:13–14; Isa. 11:15–16). Leviathan's defeat symbolizes YHWH's deliverance of the people from Babylonian exile.

Finally, Isa. 27:2–13 presents the new vineyard allegory in which YHWH finally gets the vineyard to produce fruit (cf. Isa. 5:1–7). The vineyard metaphor portrays Israel's taking root in the aftermath of exile to grow once again. With its restoration, the exiles of Israel will return from Assyria and Egypt.

The Text in the Interpretive Tradition

Many interpreters view these chapters as the so-called Isaiah Apocalypse, insofar as Isaiah 24–27 employs motifs of cosmic chaos and restoration, the resurrection of the dead (see Isa. 26:14, 19), and a view of the future that suggests the end of time. But these motifs are not necessarily apocalyptic. Like many prophetic writings, Isaiah 24–27 employs mythological motifs to portray divine action in the world (see, e.g., Amos 7–9; Isaiah 49–54; Habakkuk 3; Ezekiel 8–11), and the references to "in that day" in the passage are simple references to the future. Overall, the passage simply points to the downfall of an unnamed, exalted city of chaos (Isa. 24:10, 12; 25:2–3; 26:5), likely Babylon, which will precede the recognition of YHWH's sovereignty throughout the world.

The overthrow of Babylon, the restoration of good relations between Israel and the nations in these chapters (cf. Isa. 2:2–4), and the intertextual resignification of earlier prophetic texts in these chapters point to the late sixth century as the setting for composition, although Isa. 27:2–13 might be earlier. Isaiah 24–27 would then play an important role in binding together the prophecies of Isaiah ben Amoz in Isaiah 1–39 and those of the exilic prophet Deutero-Isaiah in Isaiah 40–55 to form a sixth-century edition of the book at the onset of Persian rule. This period saw the restoration of the Jerusalem temple with Persian support, thereby opening a new era for Jerusalem's relationship with foreign nations.

Paul cites Isa. 25:8 in his discussion of resurrection in 1 Cor. 15:54 and Isa. 27:9 in his discussion of forgiveness of sins in Rom. 11:27.

Rabbinic tradition views the city of chaos as Jerusalem and understands the entire block to be concerned with Jerusalem's restoration.

The Text in Contemporary Discussion

The twentieth century saw two major attempts by world powers to establish an international body to which nations could turn to settle conflicts. The creation of the League of Nations was the first attempt in the aftermath of World War I, and the creation of the United Nations in the aftermath of World War II was the second. Although hardly perfect, the United Nations played important roles in the creation of the modern state of Israel in 1948 and the containment of the Cold War to regional conventional conflicts rather than all-out nuclear war. Although the United Nations is frequently politicized and rendered ineffective and irrelevant by many of its member states, it still remains an important institution for achieving peace and justice in the world.

Isaiah 28–33

YHWH's Plan for Jerusalem: Announcement of a New King

The Text in Its Ancient Context

The first portion of the book of Isaiah concludes with a block of material in Isaiah 28–33 that focuses on the prophet's instruction concerning YHWH's plans for the deliverance of Jerusalem and the emergence of a new king. The oracles in this block each begin with an introductory "Woe" (Isa. 28:1; 29:1; 29:15; 30:1; 31:1; cf. 33:1), with the exception of the culminating unit in Isa. 32:1, which begins with "Behold!" This block includes five subunits, namely, Isa. 28:1–29; 29:1–24; 30:1–33; 31:1–9; and 32:1–33:24.

Isaiah 28:1–29 begins the sequence with the prophet's instruction concerning YHWH's purpose in bringing Assyrian rule. The oracle condemns the leadership of both the northern kingdom of Israel and the southern kingdom of Judah for self-indulgence, gluttony, and drunkenness, all metaphors for royal incompetence. The imagery of the covenant with death presupposes the Canaanite "marzeah." ritual, which celebrates descent into the underworld, perhaps at the outset of the dry summer season. Isaiah is well familiar with agricultural metaphor and frequently employs it to makes his points. In order to produce dill, cumin, wheat, and so on, the produce must first be crushed.

Isaiah 29:1–24 presents the prophet's instruction concerning YHWH's purpose in assaulting Jerusalem. The term Ariel, "lion of G-d," recalls the lion as symbol of the tribe of Judah (Gen. 49:8–11) and serves as a pun on the Hebrew term, *har'el*, which designates the temple altar hearth (see Ezek. 43:15–16). The first "woe" oracle in 29:1–14 portrays YHWH's "conquest" of Jerusalem with a foreign army just as David conquered it with his own soldiers (2 Sam. 5:6–9). Isaiah 29:11–12 calls on readers to view the book of Isaiah as a sealed vision. The second "woe" oracle, in 29:15–24, focuses on the realization of YHWH's purpose for Zion so that the blind and the deaf (see Isaiah 6) will sanctify YHWH.

Isaiah 30:1–33 presents the prophet's instruction concerning YHWH's delay in delivering the people from Assyria. This oracle expresses Isaiah's dissatisfaction with Hezekiah's embassy to Egypt to enlist support for his revolt against Assyria. As in Isaiah 7, the prophet opposes military alliances as a denial of the power and sovereignty of YHWH. Consequently, YHWH will delay deliverance until the people show greater trust. In the end, a teacher will arise to guide the people to throw out their idols so that YHWH will strike down Assyria. Within the context of the final form of the book of Isaiah, this would refer to Second Isaiah and his or her successors in Isaiah 40–66.

Isaiah 31:1–9 presents the prophet's warning concerning reliance on Egyptian aid in Hezekiah's revolt against Assyria. Only YHWH will protect Jerusalem much like a lion or hovering birds protect their prey.

Isaiah 32:1–33:24 concludes the sequence with a presentation of prophetic instruction concerning the future, righteous king. The first portion of this subunit, in Isa. 32:1–20, presents the prophet's vision of the righteous king whom the blind, deaf, and dumb will see when their eyes, ears, and minds are opened to YHWH's purpose (see Isaiah 6). In keeping with Isaiah's view of YHWH as the true Creator, such recognition will result in the blooming of the wilderness and the people will be secure (see Isa. 40:1–11). The second portion of this subunit, in Isa. 33:1–24, begins with a woe oracle that introduces a liturgical presentation of the new king in conjunction with the downfall of Israel's oppressor. In the end, the people who were rendered blind, deaf, and dumb in Isaiah 6 will see the king in his beauty in 33:17 and a secure Jerusalem in 33:20, in which YHWH serves as the ultimate king.

The Text in the Interpretive Tradition

Scholars have argued that most of the material in Isaiah 28–33 was written by Isaiah ben Amoz, but some elements represent later composition. The liturgical composition in Isaiah 33 appears to be the product of the final fifth-century edition of the book, in the time of Ezra and Nehemiah. Isaiah 33 closes the first portion of the book of Isaiah with a vision of the new king and the restored Jerusalem. Its liturgical character indicates that the book could have been presented as part of a temple liturgy. Isaiah 30:19–33; 32:1–8, 15–20, which points to Josiah's restoration as the projected outcome of the prophecies of Isaiah, appears to have been composed for the Josianic edition of Isaiah in the late seventh century.

The authors of the Dead Sea Scrolls apparently saw the references to the future teachers of Israel in Isa. 30:19–33 as a reference to their own Righteous Teacher who formed the group in the early second century BCE and led them to the site of Qumran, where they awaited G-d's final apocalyptic war against the wicked of the world. Although they anticipated a restoration of Jerusalem, events did not turn out as expected and both Qumran and the Jerusalem temple were destroyed in the Zealot revolt of 66–74 CE. The Great Isaiah Scroll from Qumran (1QIsa[a]) has a gap between Isaiah 33 and Isaiah 34, indicating that this is the main structural division of the book.

Many of these texts appear in the New Testament. The reference to speaking in tongues in Isa. 28:11 appears in 1 Cor. 14:21 as part of Paul's efforts to prompt the people to trust in prophets and not in those who speak in tongues. Nevertheless, Isa. 28:11–13 was influential in promoting such practice among Pentecostal and charismatic Christians (see Mark 16:17; Acts 19:6; 28:1–6; 1 Corinthians 12–14). The precious cornerstone of Isa. 28:16 appears in Paul's characterization of Torah in Rom. 9:33, and its reference to trust appears in his discussion of justification by faith in Rom. 10:11. It also appears in Peter's characterization of Scripture in 1 Pet. 2:6. The deep sleep of Isa. 29:10 appears as part of Paul's polemic against Israel in Rom. 11:8. The motif of vain worship in Isa. 29:13 appears in the polemics against Pharisees (rabbinic Jews) in Matt. 15:7 and Mark 7:6. The destruction of the wisdom of the wise in Isa. 29:14 factors into Paul's discussion of the demise of those who do not believe in Christ in 1 Cor. 1:19. The reference to the potter and the clay plays a key role in Paul's argument in Rom. 9:19–21 that humans cannot resist G-d.

Rashi read Isa. 30:19–33 as a reference to the days of the Messiah, but other medieval interpreters, such as Kimḥi, read it as a reference to Hezekiah. Rashi, Kimḥi, Ibn Ezra, and others read the righteous monarch of Isa. 32:1 as a reference to Hezekiah. The vision of the king in his beauty in Isa. 33:17 is a reference to a vision of the Shekinah, or presence of G-d, according to Rashi, although Kimḥi sees it as a reference to Hezekiah once again (for comments by Rashi, Kimḥi, Ibn Ezra, and others, see Rosenberg, ad loc.).

Isaiah 27:6–28:13; 29:22–23 functions as the Haftarah reading for Exod. 1:1–6:1. The Haftarah's themes of judgment leading to restoration thereby accompany the narrative of Israel's enslavement in Egypt with its initial promises of deliverance from Egyptian bondage.

The Text in Contemporary Discussion

YHWH's delay in bringing about the restoration of Jerusalem following the Assyrian punishment is a major factor in the conceptualization of divine action in the book of Isaiah. It becomes a means to defend the integrity of G-d in the aftermath of the Assyrian invasions; that is, the claim that Judah and Israel deserve punishment protects YHWH from charges that the deity failed to live up to the terms of the eternal covenant with the house of David and the city of Jerusalem. Indeed, the postponement of restoration until after the Babylonian exile, again after the building of the Second Temple, and even again until after the reforms of Ezra and Nehemiah, testify to the faithful vision of G-d's power, fidelity, and integrity in the book of Isaiah over against the experience of invasion, reversal, and subjugation. Such an issue is particularly important in the aftermath of the Shoah, in which we continue to ask questions about G-d's presence, morality, and power in the face of unspeakable evil. Such questions point to continued faithfulness in G-d together with a corresponding faithfulness to truth that is inseparable from our relationship with G-d. We do not yet have all the answers, but we continue to strive to achieve them.

Isaiah 34–35

Prophetic Instruction concerning YHWH's Return of Exiles to Zion

The Text in Its Ancient Context

Isaiah 34–35 introduce the second half of the book of Isaiah, in chapters 34–66, with an emphasis on the judgment of the nations, here represented by Edom, and the return of the exiles to Zion, a major concern in Isaiah 40–66. Edom is condemned in biblical literature for its role in the Babylonian destruction of Jerusalem (Ps. 137:7; Jer. 49:7–22; Lam. 4:21–22; Ezek. 25:12–17; Obadiah). Isaiah 34 presents a number of parallels with Isaiah 1: the call to attention (Isa. 1:2; 34:1); YHWH's vengeance (Isa. 1:24; 34:8); unquenchable burning (Isa. 1:24; 34:10); YHWH's mouth has spoken (Isa. 1:20; 34:16); the sword of punishment (Isa. 1:20; 34:5–6); sacrificial blood and fat (Isa. 1:11–15; 34:6–7); Sodom and Gomorrah (Isa. 1:7–10; 34:9–10); and wilting leaves (Isa. 1:30; 34:4). Isaiah 35 portrays the return of the exiles to Jerusalem as a second exodus, much like Second Isaiah.

The Text in the Interpretive Tradition

The Great Isaiah Scroll from Qumran (1QIsaiah[a]) has a gap of several lines between Isaiah 33 and Isaiah 34, indicating the fundamental structural division of the book. Various scholars have confirmed the literary division of the book at this point.

The Text in Contemporary Discussion

The recollection of the exodus in Isaiah 35 points to one of the most important holidays in Judaism, the Passover, which celebrates the exodus from Egypt. The exodus is recounted each year at the Passover seder, a home dinner service that celebrates Jewish freedom from oppression and return to the land of Israel. The appearance of this motif in

Isaiah 35—and indeed throughout the entire book of Isaiah—points to the importance of the Passover observance in antiquity as well as in modern times.

Isaiah 36–39

Narratives concerning YHWH's Deliverance of Jerusalem and Hezekiah

The Text in Its Ancient Context

The Hezekiah narratives found in Isaiah 36–39 also appear in 2 Kings 18–20, albeit it in somewhat different form. Because these chapters contain the last references to the prophet Isaiah ben Amoz in the book of Isaiah, many interpreters presume that they form an appendix to an early form of the book that focuses only on the eighth-century prophet. More recent discussion has recognized the transitional function of these chapters as the concluding reference to the Babylonian exile in Isaiah 39, which points forward to the so-called Second Isaiah, beginning in Isaiah 40. Overall, these chapters point to YHWH's deliverance of Jerusalem as a result of Hezekiah's turning to YHWH, which anticipates the calls for recognition of YHWH's deliverance at the end of the Babylonian exile in the second part of the book.

Isaiah 36–37 presents the account of YHWH's deliverance of Jerusalem during the 701-BCE siege of the city by the Assyrian monarch Sennacherib. Following the unexpected death in battle of Sargon II in 705, King Hezekiah of Judah and Prince Merodach Baladan of Babylon planned a two-pronged revolt against Assyria. Sennacherib proved able to meet the challenge, and conquered Tyre in his initial counterattack in 701. With the fall of Tyre, Hezekiah's western allies abandoned him, leaving Judah open to Assyrian attack. The Assyrian army overran Judah, destroying the city of Lachish and all other cities in Judah while laying siege to Jerusalem. When the Assyrian Rab Shakeh, chief cupbearer (a high administrative title), demanded Jerusalem's unconditional surrender, Hezekiah spread the document before YHWH in the temple and appealed for help. Isaiah answered on YHWH's behalf, indicating that YHWH would deliver Jerusalem due to Hezekiah's faithfulness. According to the account, YHWH's angel killed 185,000 Assyrian troops, and Sennacherib himself was assassinated by his own sons in the temple of his god, Nisroch. Sennacherib's records, however, claim that he forced the capitulation of Hezekiah, and returned to Assyria with many captives and much booty. He was assassinated by his sons some twenty years later, in 681 BCE. Scholars argue that Sennacherib was compelled to negotiate a settlement with Hezekiah that left Jerusalem intact and Hezekiah alive so that he could move against Merodach Baladan in Babylonia. As a result, both Hezekiah and Sennacherib claimed victory.

Isaiah 38 presents the account of Hezekiah's recovery from illness prior to the revolt. Again, the narrative stresses YHWH's response when the king turns to YHWH. The Isaian account includes Hezekiah's prayer, which is absent in the Kings narrative, to accentuate Hezekiah's faith in YHWH.

Isaiah 39 recounts the embassy of Merodach Baladan to Hezekiah in preparation for the revolt. Isaiah opposed Hezekiah's revolt and condemned Hezekiah's willingness to ally with the Babylonians, arguing that someday his sons would be carried off as captives to Babylon.

The Text in the Interpretive Tradition

As noted above, many scholars recognize that Isaiah 36–39 serves as a transitional narrative within the book of Isaiah as a whole. The concluding reference to Babylonian exile in Isaiah 39 anticipates the return from Babylonian exile beginning in Isaiah 40. Hezekiah's faithfulness therefore serves as a model for the response of the exiles to YHWH in the second part of the book. But the Hezekiah narratives also function as a means to contrast Hezekiah with the presentation of Ahaz in Isaiah 7.

Ahaz rejects Isaiah's calls for him to trust in YHWH and sees Jerusalem subjugated to the Assyrians as a result, but Hezekiah turns to

YHWH during the revolt and sees the deliverance of the city from the Assyrian siege. Interpreters note the location of Isaiah's encounter with Ahaz at the conduit of the Upper Pool by the Fuller's Field in Isaiah 7, and that the Assyrian Rab Shakeh stands at the same location when demanding the surrender of Jerusalem in Isaiah 36–37. When compared with the Hezekiah narratives in 2 Kings 18–20, differences in the text (e.g., the inclusion of the prayer of Hezekiah in Isaiah 38) indicate that Hezekiah appears far more pious and faithful in the Isaian version than in Kings, where Hezekiah immediately submits to Sennacherib at the outset of 2 Kings 18. Overall, the Isaian text presents Hezekiah as a repentant monarch who turns to YHWH in time of crisis.

The Text in Contemporary Discussion

The Hezekiah narratives demonstrate the importance of accounting for literary and theological perspective in the interpretation of biblical literature. Although Isaiah 36–39 claims a great victory for Hezekiah, Sennacherib's records also claim a great victory for the Assyrians. Indeed, both were correct; Sennacherib forced Hezekiah's submission, and both Hezekiah and Jerusalem survived the Assyrian onslaught. Such a lesson should be borne in mind when reading biblical literature in general. When the prophets claim that Israel was punished with exile because the people sinned, does this mean that Israel actually committed sins that justified national catastrophe? Or is this a means to explain disaster as an act of G-d and thereby to defend the power, presence, and righteousness of G-d in the world when disaster strikes? In the aftermath of the Shoah (Holocaust), modern theologians continue to struggle with the notion that human suffering must be explained by human sin.

WORKS CITED

Blenkinsopp, Joseph. 2000. *Isaiah 1–39*. AB 19. New York: Doubleday.

Childs, Brevard S. 2001. *Isaiah: A Commentary*. OTL. Louisville: Westminster John Knox.

Erlandsson, Seth. 1970. *The Burden of Babylon: A Study of Isaiah 13:2–14:23*. ConBOT 4. Lund: Gleerup.

Evans, Craig A. 1988. "On the Unity and Parallel Structure of the Book of Isaiah," *VT* 38:129–47.

Fohrer, Georg. 1962. "Jesaja 1 als Zusammenfassung der Verkündigung Jesajas." *ZAW* 74:251–68.

Kaiser, Otto. 1983. *Isaiah 1–12: A Commentary*. OTL. Philadelphia: Westminster.

Kaplan, Mordecai. 1926. "Isaiah 6:1–11." *JBL* 45:251–59.

Rosenberg, A. J. 1982–1983. *The Book of Isaiah*. Judaica Books of the Bible. New York: Judaica.

Schäfer, Peter. 1998. *Judeophobia: Attitudes towards the Jews in the Ancient World*. Cambridge, MA: Harvard University Press.

Sweeney, Marvin A. 1996. *Isaiah 1–39, with an Introduction to Prophetic Literature*. FOTL 16. Grand Rapids: Eerdmans.

___________. 2008. *Reading the Hebrew Bible after the Shoah: Engaging Holocaust Theology*. Minneapolis: Fortress Press.

Tomasino, A. J. 1993. "Isaiah 1.1–2.4 and 63–66 and the Composition of the Isaianic Corpus." *JSOT* 57:81–98.

Tucker, Gene M. 2001. "Isaiah." In *The New Interpreter's Bible*, edited by Leander E. Keck, 6:25–305. Nashville: Abingdon.

Tull, Patricia K. 2010. *Isaiah 1–39*. Smyth and Helwys Bible Commentary. Macon, GA: Smyth & Helwys.

Wiesel, Elie. 1982. *Souls on Fire: Portraits and Legends of Hasidic Masters*. New York: Vintage.

Isaiah 40–66

Chris A. Franke

Introduction

The book of Isaiah deals with people, places, and events spanning several centuries, from 733 BCE to some time around 515 BCE. Chapters 1–39, referred to as First or Proto-Isaiah, focus on the time when Israel and Judah were under Assyrian rule. An ominous message to King Hezekiah announces the rise of the Babylonian Empire in Isaiah 39. The result is that nothing will be left of his kingdom, Judah, and his Davidic lineage will come to an end. The backdrop of the following chapters, 40–66, includes the Babylonian destruction of Judah and the exile of many of its citizens in 587 BCE; the rise of the Persian Empire under Cyrus the Great in 539 BCE; and the restoration of life in Jerusalem after Cyrus allowed all exiles to return home. While the name Isaiah never appears in 40–66, Isaiah 1–39 and 40–66 share common features, including emphasis on Jerusalem/Zion, reference to the Davidic monarchy, and common images and names of God.

Chapters 40–66 treat two different eras. Chapters 40–55 are addressed to exiles living in Babylon during the rule of Cyrus (538–515 BCE). Their liberation from Babylonian oppression is soon to come. Chapters 56–66 recount the situation in the newly formed Judah, now called Yehud, after the exiles return home and are united with those who had remained in the land after the fall of the kingdom.

Chapters 40–55 are usually identified as Second or Deutero-Isaiah and 56–66 as Third or Trito-Isaiah. Scholars disagree about the authorship of these two sections of the book of Isaiah. Some hold that they represent two different authors or prophets. The mostly hopeful messages of Deutero-Isaiah (abbreviated as DI) and its Babylonian setting are very different from the more somber and sometimes threatening tone and setting in Yehud of Trito-Isaiah (abbreviated as TI). Others see continuity between the two. The strongest defense of single authorship is the consistent literary style throughout. A geographical change does not in itself warrant asserting a new author. In this article, the book of Isaiah is abbreviated as BOI. DI indicates chapters 40–55 and TI chapters 56–66. The view here asserts a single authorial voice.

Other suggestions describing the authorship of DI include the following. Ulrich Berges proposes that cultic representatives are the authorial group responsible for the composition of 40–55 (Berges, 587–88). The people who were sent into exile after the destruction of Jerusalem surely included the priests familiar with temple worship and other cultic activities. They could also be responsible for composition of prayers and/or psalms used in worship.

Lena-Sofia Tiemeyer (26–30) proposes the possibility of female authorship of 40–55. In support of this view, she cites the many metaphors that compare God to a woman, the references to female sociosexual roles, descriptions of tasks related to motherhood, and the absence of negative images of women.

Isaiah 40:1–31

Israel's God Is Incomparable

The Text in Its Ancient Context

Chapter 40 is the beginning of another major section of the BOI. It represents momentous changes of time, place, and mood from chapters 1–39, which are set in mid- to late eighth-century Jerusalem. The time and place of Isaiah 40–55 is 539 BCE, when Babylonia succumbed to Cyrus the Great of Persia. DI's message is addressed to the community of exiles living in Babylon. The chapter begins with words of comfort and reassurance and promises change for those living under Babylonian rule (40:1–2).

What is known about the exiles who lived in Babylonian territory? Some scholars describe their living conditions as relatively benign. Life continued in exile with little if any disadvantage to the exiles. However, data from sociological and psychological sciences reveal a very different view of people forcibly removed from a secure existence in their homeland. Living as minorities in a foreign country offered little if any security or civil rights. "The Judean experience of deportation . . . was a severe and traumatic personal, social, and psychological event" (Moore and Kelle, 364). Convincing people who suffered under such conditions for half a century that God was on their side would have been a difficult task. They would need constant and reliable reassurance that God is aware of their existence. DI not only acknowledges their long term of suffering but in a stunning admission also acknowledges that they "received from YHWH's hand" twice as much punishment as they deserved for their sins. Their fortunes are soon to be reversed. A way will be prepared in the wilderness, and God will lead them back home.

Isaiah 40–66 is filled with a variety of images demonstrating YHWH's power and will to save. The long poem in 40:12–31 is the first of many such demonstrations. The prominent image of God in these verses is of a powerful, all-knowing, everlasting Creator. The literary device of the rhetorical question is used here and elsewhere in DI. It often appears in connection with repetition, another technique by which DI gets the attention of the audience: "To whom then will you liken God?" (40:18) and "To whom then will you compare me?" (40:25). The intent is not to demand answers of the audience but to assert the obvious. No one can be compared to YHWH. YHWH is incomparable. The author takes an argumentative or polemical tone. The defensive aspect of the polemic is because the other side of the issue is all too obvious to the audience. They have good reason to doubt.

The Text in the Interpretive Tradition

Anyone who has ever listened to Handel's *Messiah* will be familiar with the BOI. The libretto contains seventeen citations from the BOI (Davies, 464–84). The Messiah to whom Handel points is Jesus as described in the Synoptic Gospels. Mark's Gospel begins with an allusion to the BOI, showing John the Baptist preparing way of the Lord (Mark 1:2–3). Since the New Testament cites the BOI more times than any other Old Testament text, it is not surprising that Handel's librettist, Charles Jennens, used numerous texts from Isaiah. The librettist repeats Isa. 40:1–5 almost word for word in the first three pieces. The only phrase omitted is the troubling "double payment from the LORD for all her sins." Other citations from Isaiah 40 in the *Messiah* include 40:9, which describes the messenger who brings the good news, and 40:11, describing God the shepherd gently leading the lambs.

The Text in Contemporary Discussion

The frequent use of motifs and ideas from the BOI in the New Testament and later Christian interpretations has led many Christians to believe that the only way to understand Isaiah is through a christological lens. Knowledge of events in Israel's history as well as an awareness of how these texts were used well before New Testament times is crucial to a wider view of the importance of the BOI. From early on in Jewish tradition, selections from Isaiah 40–60 that recall the destruction of the temple and the exile from Judah were read in synagogues before the high holy days (Paul, 71). The message of comfort in 40:1 is the first of these readings, which mark the period of personal and national mourning for Jews. Sabbath readings in current Jewish liturgy are filled with selections from the book of Isaiah. Both Jewish and Christian traditions have appropriated texts from Second Isaiah for liturgical use.

Isaiah 41:1–44:8

The Nations and Their Gods Are Put on Trial/God Reassures Israel

The Text in Its Ancient Context

DI has been called the "spider poet" because of the tangled web of connections found throughout 40–55 (Kim, 178). Chapters 41:1–44:8

illustrate this phenomenon. Motifs include the nations, the making of idols, Israel/Jacob as God's chosen, the servant, and transformation of the wilderness. Many of these motifs appear throughout the rest of 40–66. God is portrayed as warrior, attorney or judge, a woman giving birth, king, comforter. Literary genres adapted from ancient Near Eastern documents include terminology reflecting a courtroom trial, hymns used in liturgies, and rhetorical questions, all of which would be familiar to DI's audience in Babylon.

Isaiah 41 begins with a courtroom setting. God puts the nations on trial, demanding proof that they and their deities are powerful. Are they able to control events, predict the future? Do they have power enough to terrify or harm others? As evidence that it is YHWH who is able to control events, predict the future, and terrify nations, God has called up Cyrus the Persian king to defeat the Babylonian Empire in 539 BCE. The gods are unable to prove that they can control and predict the future. They remain silent and ineffectual in contrast to God's powerful acts on behalf of Jacob/Israel. A distinctive feature in this section is God speaking in the first person, emphatically asserting that "I have held my peace, I have kept still," "I will cry out," "I will lay waste mountains," "I will turn the rivers into islands," "I will lead the blind," "I will turn the darkness before them into light," "these are the things I will do," "I will not forsake them" (Isa. 42:14–16). An English translation of 41:1–44:8 reveals over 130 occurrences of first-person pronouns.

The courtroom scene in 43:9–13 brings a new and far more serious challenge to the nations. They have no witnesses who can prove that their gods exist. The nations were initially asked to show that they and their gods were powerful. YHWH now asserts that

> *before me no god was formed,*
> *nor will there be any after me. (43:10)*

thus denying the nature or existence of the gods.

While the nations tremble with fright, YHWH comforts Jacob/ Israel: "Do not fear, for I am with you" (43:5). The "fear not" formula appears throughout DI, beginning with God's opening message to the exiles (40:9). It underlies the prophet's message in 41:1–44:8. The phrase "fear not" is adapted from an ancient Near Eastern literary-theological motif used to indicate that the gods support their kings and people. Shalom Paul cites an example of the goddess Ishtar reassuring Assyrian kings that she will deliver their enemies for destruction (Paul, 166). Also familiar in these documents is the phrase "grasping the right hand," which demonstrates that a king or god supports his people. DI uses this formula in 41:10 and 13 to indicate divine support.

The hymn of praise in 42:10–12 is a familiar genre frequently used in their worship services. All are commanded to lift up their voices and sing to give glory to YHWH and declare God's praise! The hymn genre most likely originated in a cultic setting. When a group of people gathers to worship, part of their worship includes praying and singing. Motifs for these prayers include complaint, lament, and thanksgiving, which are used in Isaiah 40–66. All of these genres reflect significant events with which the audience was familiar. These features will immediately direct the audience's attention to the significance or tone of the message.

The Text in the Interpretive Tradition

Scholars reading Isaiah 40–66 over the years have proposed a wide variety of strategies to understand its complicated features. One of the most significant contributions to understanding the literary dimensions of DI was made by James Muilenburg in his commentary in *The Interpreter's Bible.* Using the results of form-critical studies of Isaiah 40–66, he showed that the prophet used typical forms of the time but tweaked them, adding to or altering the formulas to give new depth and nuance to the message.

The cult of the Babylonian gods is described in some detail beginning in Isa. 41:6–7. DI emphasizes idolatry and especially the construction of images of Babylonian deities in chapters 40–47. The disparaging polemics against the construction and worship of statues is evidence that the exiles in Babylon were familiar with and perhaps attracted to these practices. Accentuated here is YHWH's power over nations, kings, and their deities; the idea that YHWH is "the first and the last"; and the idea that "there is no god besides me" and "no savior besides me."

Some have referred to DI as the exponent of monotheism in Israel. While one might speak of incipient monotheism in DI, it is not so much a question of how many gods there are but rather what kind of a god YHWH is. Israel's repeated attention to a single deity over the course of their history is the background of the later development of a full-fledged monotheism. See Mark Smith's discussions of this fascinating and complicated aspect of Israelite history and religion (Smith 1990; 2001).

The Text in Contemporary Discussion

The BOI often uses the metaphor of regeneration of land, plant life, and waters and compares these to the condition of human existence. The repeated references to life-giving water in DI and TI reflect the devastated conditions of the land reduced to a wasteland by the ravages of war. Recent interest in ecological issues has encouraged Bible scholars to address this issue.

Patricia K. Tull brings these issues to her study of Isaiah, demonstrating that Isaiah uses "plant imagery to tie human spiritual and societal health to environmental well-being" (Tull, 27). She indicates that it is sometimes impossible to tell when the text is to be understood literally or metaphorically. Referring to a group of farmers who studied Genesis 3, she cites their observation that "when humans are disconnected from God, the soil will be the first to suffer."

Isaiah 44:9–20

The Folly of Making and Worshiping Images of Deities

The Text in Its Ancient Context

Scattered through Isaiah 40–48 are references to features of Babylonian religion, especially the making and use of images of gods in the Babylonian pantheon. DI's perspective on images, artisans who make them, and those who worship them is consistently negative and critical. Isaiah 44:9–20 features a detailed description of the construction of *images* or *idols* (for DI the terms are synonymous), from the planting of the trees used for carvings to the iron workshop in which images are forged. The tone of this anti-idol passage is scathing sarcasm and ridicule. DI derides those who burn wood to cook their meals and warm their hands and then bow down to a statue made of the same kind of wood. Such a person is a "shepherd of ashes with a deluded mind" (44:20, author's trans.).

A recent commentary by Shalom Paul is a rich source of background information for Babylonian history, literature, religion, and culture during the time of the formation of Isaiah 40–66. Paul describes an event during the reign of Babylonian king Nabonidus, who made dramatic changes in the Babylonian cult. One of the most significant was to change the order of the gods in the pantheon. The chief god Marduk was deposed and replaced with another god. Nabonidus also canceled celebration of a religious holiday, which enraged the populace. Marduk's priests, understandably upset, published a document attacking Nabonidus's behavior, claiming that he "looks at representations [of the gods] and utters blasphemies" (Paul, 13).

DI's familiarity with the Babylonian scene is clear from the details included in the anti-idol passages. He takes for granted that his audience living under Babylonian rule for decades is familiar with these practices. Understood in light of the political situation in Babylon, it is not difficult to understand DI's polemical tone. In the words of DI, Marduk's "devotees shall be put to shame" (44:11) when their emperor deposed their chief god. Critique of the gods is critique of Babylonian politics. DI's exilic audience would relish the disarray of Babylonian's inept and divided leadership.

The Text in the Interpretive Tradition

DI uses satire in several poems that describe Babylonian practices and politics; for example, Isaiah 46–47. *Satire* is used to ridicule, diminish, or attack an individual, an institution, or a culture. It evokes in the audience feelings of scorn or contempt for the subject. Putting the drudgery of the artisans in elegant, poetic language heightens the level of ridicule and mockery. Some consider this literary feature to be beneath the soaring language of DI. However, reading it in light of oppressive conditions in Babylonia makes DI's satirical critique a fit way to disempower an oppressive empire.

The Text in Contemporary Discussion

What significance might this satire on images of deities have for diverse religious groups? Orthodoxy has a tradition of the veneration of icons. The veneration of the Bible itself is a traditional practice for some Christians. Hindu practices include processions of images of deities as part of its tradition. Another way to reflect on this question is to ask: How is the divine made present in the world?

"Laughing at Idols" is the title of an article by George M. Soares-Prabhu (1995, 110), who critiques DI's ridiculing the Babylonian practice of making statues of their gods. He interprets Isa. 44:9–20 from his perspective of religion and politics in India, where many world religions exist "in tolerable harmony," and contrasts this with DI's "inadequate view of God." Soares-Prabhu highlights the value of pluralist Indian interpretations as a corrective to intolerance often seen in Western religions, which emphasize monotheism. Familiarity with interpretations of the Bible from the perspective of the social location of the reader opens up the richness of the biblical text for all cultures.

Isaiah 44:21–45:24

A Reminder to Israel—You Will Be Created and Freed by God

The Text in Its Ancient Context

The message of hope in 44:1–6 is resumed in verse 21 after the polemic against the image makers. DI again asserts that, while they cannot predict the future, predictions made by God's messengers will be fulfilled. The ruins of Jerusalem and other cities of Judah will be rebuilt and repopulated (44:26), and the foundation of the new temple will be laid (44:28). As proof that this will happen, DI introduces Cyrus, king of Persia, who has defeated the hapless Nabonidus, ruler of Babylonia. God's purpose will be carried out by Cyrus, who YHWH calls "my shepherd" (44:28).

It must be kept in mind that the audience for these messages is the exiles living in Babylonia under Babylonian rule. They are familiar with the Babylonian scene. They know about the coming of Cyrus, the fall of Nabonidus, and would also be familiar with the form and style of official messages about Babylonian kings. The motif of rebuilding cities and their temples is often attributed to kings in Mesopotamian documents (Paul, 247). To get the attention of this audience, DI uses a variety of examples with which the exiles would be familiar.

One of the most deeply disturbing ideas for the exiles was the loss of the Davidic monarchy and the temple. God's promise of the permanence of these institutions had been broken. DI explains that God's covenant promise of an eternal Davidic line continues through Cyrus, who now takes on David's title as "the anointed one" (45:1). As a caution to those who are critical of a foreigner as the anointed one, DI makes several striking comparisons. God is a potter, and the critics are the clay pots. The potter asks if the clay can criticize its maker. In two other images, God is a father and a mother. The critics are again asked if anyone questions their parents about who they are making. No answer is needed: the critics' position is ridiculous. To dispel further objections, God announces that Cyrus "will build my city and set my exiles free" (45:13).

The Text in the Interpretive Tradition

The ramifications of the assertion that God is sole creator of all things are far reaching. God can make Cyrus king and can strip other kings of their robes, signs of their power. For DI, the belief that God is one can result in only one conclusion: all nations will "follow you," "bow down to you," "come over in chains," and must admit that "God is with you alone" (45:14). This is described as a "fantasy nourished by resentment at subjection to the great powers" (Blenkinsopp, 262). Such a sentiment can be understood by any people at any time who live under the oppression of a powerful empire.

The Text in Contemporary Discussion

Bible scholar Ada María Isasi-Díaz speaks of her experience living in exile from Cuba and her yearning to return home lest she forget her own country (Isasi-Díaz, 149–63). She found solace and understanding in Psalm 137, a lament of exiles yearning for their homeland. This psalm asks God to remember the fall of Jerusalem. It includes the desire for vengeance against the enemy, much like that against Babylon in Isa. 45:13–14, and expresses the wish that the babies of the enemies will be dashed against the rock. Isasi-Díaz asks: What is the theology behind this psalm?

Her personal experiences influence how she reads such texts. Seeing injustice against the poor and experiencing the effects of sexism in her church and ethnic prejudice as a Cuban living in America shaped her hermeneutical strategy. Rather than trying to read a text "objectively," that is, trying to come to the original meaning of the text, she realized the importance of clarifying her own perspective and her purpose for reading that text. She emphasizes the three-way relationship between "the reader, the writer, and the text." A reader's questions influence what the text could have meant in the past and what it means today. She describes her approach to the text as "oppression-liberation."

The language of Psalm 137 and Isa. 45:13–14 can express both personal and community grief for suffering terrible losses, including the loss of order in their world. Isasi-Díaz, while uncomfortable with the strong and vengeful sentiments, prays this psalm because it has a cathartic effect. It allows her to express a troubling feeling. She also notes that there is a great difference between words of vengeance and acts of vengeance.

Isaiah 46:1–13

Babylonian Street Scene—A Procession of Idols Carried on Beasts of Burden

The Text in Its Ancient Context

Chapter 46 is the polar opposite of the triumphant march of the exiles returning home in Isaiah 40. Bel and Nebo, chief gods of Babylonia, are carried in an ignominious procession out of their homeland into captivity. One of the motifs in previous chapters has been the folly of making images and worshiping them. This begins in 40:18–20 and is repeated in every succeeding chapter.

This scene in 46:1–7 would have been familiar to the exiles in Babylon. On the occasion of the New Year festival, the images of Bel and Nebo were carried in a procession through the streets. Bel is a title for the god Marduk, Babylon's protector. Nebo was his son, who during the New Year celebration was to write down the fate of the cities for the coming year. A very different occasion in Mesopotamian culture was transporting images of gods out of a threatened or destroyed city. Yet another example was seizure of the statues by the conquering enemy. This was done for economic reasons, to confiscate the precious metals and stones set in the statues. It also mocked the impotency of gods of the defeated nation.

Chapter 46 describes the gods as heavy loads on weary animals. They all stoop and stumble and bow down. The phrase "bow down" can refer to obeisance to a high authority, such as a king, or an act of worship of a god. But here it highlights their utter ineffectuality and proves that they are unable to "save" or "deliver" anyone. God addresses Jacob/Israel, emphasizing that, unlike these statues, which can save no one, "*I* carried you from the beginning." "*I* made," "*I* will bear," "*I* will carry," "*I* will save" (46:3–4). Furthermore, God accuses them of being "rebels." Here, as elsewhere in these anti-idolatry passages, the offenders are rebellious Israel. God reminds them,

> *I am God, and there is no other;*
> *I am God, and there is no one like me. (46:9)*

This recalls the infamous first idol-making event at the foot of Mount Sinai, when people worshiped the golden calf as their god (Exod. 32:1–14). YHWH initially threatened extermination of the community but relented from this plan.

Chapter 46 contrasts the downward spiral of Bel and Nebo and their supporters with the elevation of YHWH, who insists that "I will fulfill my intention" to a "stubborn" and perhaps unconvinced group of exiles. YHWH's word has been spoken; deliverance is at hand.

The Text in the Interpretive Tradition

Previous scholarship approached DI (as well as other prophetic texts) with the idea that it was made up of conventional genres, short units that originated in the spoken word. In the process of writing, these shorter units were thought to have been brought together to connect similar themes or motifs. However, the poetry of DI transcends more traditional techniques and adds nuance to conventional formulas (Franke 1994, 263). An example of the literary genius of this prophet/poet is the image of procession to contrast the fate of Jacob/Israel and that of their captors. Procession for the enemies in 46:1–2 means going into captivity. In Isaiah 47, deposed Babylon falls from her throne to earth, down to the underworld. Processions for the exiles will lead them out of captivity back to their homeland in 40:3–5; 48:20–21; and 51:9–52:2. This extended image is an essential aspect of the prophet's message to the exiles; it is far more than a mere assemblage of loosely related themes.

The Text in Contemporary Discussion

While DI's message is often characterized as a message of comfort and consolation to those living under Babylonian rule, a crucial element in chapter 46 is the accusation against Jacob/Israel of idolatry, and warnings of the consequences. Just as Isaiah 40 begins with comfort to the disconsolate, it also includes a brief polemic against idolatry, accusing the audience of comparing God to an idol made by human hands. In many of the anti-idolatry sections in DI, the issue is not denying the existence of God. The offense is comparing God to idols or considering them equals to Israel's God. The prophet's audience is not Babylonians. It is the exiles living in Babylon who have taken on the religious practices of their captors.

Isaiah 47:1–15

The Fall of Virgin Daughter Babylon

The Text in Its Ancient Context

Chapter 47 is a pivot on which the main ideas and message of DI turn (Franke 1991). In the previous chapters, the disconsolate exiles lived in fear of their conquerors, doubted that God could or would come to their rescue, needed constant encouragement that they had not been forgotten, and wondered if they were still being punished for their infidelities. DI describes numerous examples of differences between the god of Jacob and the gods of the Babylonian Empire in 40–46. The critique of the Babylonian images and especially the artisans who made them pervades this section. While YHWH was powerful and carried the people, the Babylonian deities could not even move but had to be carried by those who worshiped them.

Here God speaks directly to "virgin daughter Babylon." In the ancient world, cities were often described figuratively as women needing protection of kings. In satirical language, God ridicules all of Babylon's claims. She thought: she'd be queen forever; she was secure; she'd never be widowed; and she would never lose her children. She thought she could hide her evil deeds. She thought her astrologers could predict her future or use magic to control events.

From the beginning words in 47:1, it is clear that Babylon's future will be grim. Instead of being seated on a throne, she will sit in the dust, on the ground. Even more, she will go into "darkness," intimating her passage to the underworld.

To Babylon's humiliation, she will be stripped of her garments: veil and robe will be removed, legs uncovered. In summary, her "nakedness" and "shame" will be seen by all. The latter terms indicate exposure of her genitalia. For her crimes—showing no mercy to the exiles and especially abusing the elderly—there will be no one to save her. Just as the Babylonian deities in chapter 46 bowed down and went into captivity, so Virgin Daughter Babylon will exchange her royal status for that of slavery.

This poem has features similar to satirical laments for the dead elsewhere in Isaiah (14:3–21), as well as in lamenting the death of gods in ancient Near Eastern literature (Anderson, 60–82). These laments include the hubris of the gods or nations in their belief that they will rule forever. They also fall from their thrones, sit on the ground, and descend into the underworld.

The Text in the Interpretive Tradition

The fall of Babylon has been interpreted from the perspective of anthropology as a rite of passage (Kruger). The various details of Babylon's passage—loss of status, the shame of removing her garments and exposure, doing menial work—portray her as a queen turned slave. This description is an example of a sociocultural antitype of Babylon's status as queen. It can also be read as an antitype of the status of Jerusalem/Zion. Later chapters describe the elevation of Zion's status from widow to bride, rejected and captive to redeemed, and barren to mother of many. DI uses the fall of Babylon as a contrast to the rise of Jerusalem.

The Text in Contemporary Discussion

In chapter 47, Babylon is portrayed as the object of God's punishment. She is subjected to physical abuse and punishment, which strips her of her power. She loses her husband and children and remains alone with no one to save her. How are readers today to understand this in a meaningful way? What theological problems does such a view create?

One of the most significant challenges in reading the Bible in the modern world is how to deal with the ancient Near Eastern view of women that pervades biblical texts. In the ancient world, women were viewed as the property of men. It was commonly accepted that the ideal male was powerful, able to provide his city/family with food, shelter, and protection. Sexual fidelity is not included in the list for men. The ideal female was submissive, in need of protection, faithful to her spouse. Women were the property of their male protector, husband or father or brother. They were second-class citizens at best.

In recent years, scholars have discussed this question by providing important background information to the origins of this point of view. The *Women's Bible Commentary*, now in its third edition (Newsom, Ringe, and Lapsley), provides data to support the need of a more informed view of this matter in biblical texts, both Old and New Testament.

It is no longer justifiable for interpreters to take the biblical view of women and men as acceptable views for the world today. Citing biblical views about women out of context is not sufficient evidence to draw conclusions and make rules for society today. It is not only insufficient but also damaging to both women and men. In this matter as well as many others, a contextual view of society and culture is essential to understand values and practices in the Bible.

Isaiah 48:1–22

God Warns Israel and Announces a New Exodus

The Text in Its Ancient Context

In this chapter, several literary techniques are used by the author/editor to make connections to earlier sections, and also to segue to following material. Chapter 48 links chapters 40–47 and 49–55 by motifs or themes. These include God as Creator, Holy One of Israel, Redeemer. Cyrus, identified as "the one whom YHWH loves," is the ruler who will defeat Babylon. God declares past and future events to Jacob/Israel to demonstrate the power and reliability of the divine word over against the lifeless idols and images. However, exiles persist in their stubbornness and obstinacy.

A striking feature amid these accusations against intransigent Jacob/Israel is the depth of God's passionate reaction to their treachery. God's response is mixed. On the one hand, the people's infidelity enrages God almost to the point of exterminating them. God's reputation is at stake, only deferring from punishing them "for my name's sake," "for my own sake." God is incredulous at their behavior: "Why should my name be profaned?" (48:9–11). On the other hand, God speaks as a teacher or parent "who teaches you for your own good," observing wistfully that things would have been different if only "you had paid attention to my commandments" (48:17–19).

In the final verses (48:20–21), DI urges the audience to "go out from Babylon, flee from Chaldea" and reminds them of the exodus from Egypt. This recalls 40:1, the good news of a "highway for our God" on which they would be led through the wilderness. Øystein Lund (227–29) shows that 48:17–22 returns to several key themes in 40:12–40: YHWH's knowledge of the future and power over military and/or political events. The repetition of words or motifs at the beginning and end of a section is called an inclusio. It is a structuring device to indicate the beginning and end of a section within a text. It functions much like chapter divisions do in books today. Chapter 48 is a turning point in the direction of Isaiah 40–55. The terse statement in 48:22—"no peace for the wicked"—also points to the very end of the BOI, since it anticipates similar threatening sentiments in 57:21 and 66:24.

The Text in the Interpretive Tradition

Scholars refer to Isaiah 48 as the "problem child" of biblical criticism because of its range of motifs, grammatical peculiarities, contradictions in God's past and present actions, and excessive repetition. Some of God's actions are harsh and seemingly contradictory to the message of consolation with which DI begins. Scholars vary wildly in their assessment of this chapter. A form-critical approach fails to solve the problems. One proposal asserts that certain material was added by another writer or editor. Another eliminates repetitious features.

In a commentary that stands outside the prevailing thought of most Isaiah scholarship in the first half of the twentieth century, Charles Cutler Torrey (372–80) views Isaiah 48 as an integrated whole. It begins and ends on a note of rebuke and acknowledges that Israel, though unworthy, is the chosen people. Torrey also notes a close connection in time between the composition of Isaiah 46 and 47, as well as to motifs throughout Isaiah 40–66.

The Text in Contemporary Discussion

Chapter 48, more than any other chapter in the BOI, deals with Israel's relationship with God in all its permutations. It highlights the tension between Israel's dependence on God and its obduracy to God's word. Walter Brueggemann sees this originating in "the tension deep within the character of Yahweh" (Brueggemann, 100), speaking of the motifs of displacement and restoration that underlie Isaiah 48. He applies this to our own Western culture with the disappearance of certitude and the difficulties of maintaining a social infrastructure.

From one perspective, the problem is God's credibility and dependability. From another, it is the people of God. Rémi Lack describes the problem well: the only obstacle to salvation is the apathy of the people and their refusal to accept that a foreigner, Cyrus, is the instrument of that salvation (Lack, 106).

Works such as Brueggemann's and Lack's, which read the BOI as an integrated whole, are examples of canonical readings. This method of exegesis is a more recent development in biblical scholarship, which offers yet another way to read and understand complicated biblical texts.

Isaiah 49:1–52:12

Daughter Zion, the Servant, and the Role of the Nations in Judah's Future

Chapter 49 begins a new section of DI. Previous characters and places important in Isaiah 40–48—Cyrus as God's anointed, the artisans and their ineffectual statues, and Babylon—are no longer mentioned. The word pair Jacob/Israel occurs for the last time in 49:5–6 and is replaced by Jerusalem/Zion. Key figures—Zion/Jerusalem, the nations, and the servant—are intertwined in 49:1–52:12. These three figures are treated in three separate sections.

Zion/Jerusalem

The Text in Its Ancient Context

A major emphasis in Isaiah 49–55 is on Zion/Jerusalem. From the beginning of DI, the biggest challenge was to convince the exiles that God is not only willing to save them but also has the power to do so. The message of comfort and consolation with which DI begins (40:1) is repeated in 49:13; 51:3, 12. However, Zion remains unconvinced by these claims. YHWH has abandoned and forgotten her (49:14). The term "abandoned" is often used of a husband leaving his wife. Zion challenges God in 51:9 to "Awake, awake, put on strength!" Isaiah scholar Luis Schökel describes 51:9–52:6 as a "bold and affectionate dialogue" between Zion and her husband (Schökel, 179).

The first words God uses to answer Zion's accusation relate to Zion as a wife and mother. The most convincing argument is the image of a mother's relationship to her child. God asks a rhetorical question, "Can a mother forget her nursing child or show no compassion for the child of her womb?" (49:15). The motifs of mother and child and wife continue through to 49:26. God promises that soon Zion will have so many children that she will need a bigger tent in which to live. God reminds Zion that "you are my people" (51:16). God responds to Zion by mirroring her previous command to "wake up" and orders her to "rouse yourself," "wake up," and "depart!" Captive Jerusalem must rise from the dust, remove the bonds from her neck, and garb herself in festive apparel. Her redemption is at hand.

The Text in the Interpretive Tradition

It has long been clear that the Bible is filled with many images of God as male: king, warrior, husband, father. However, the increase of women scholars in biblical studies has given rise to a wider context for interpreting texts. Much of the terminology in chapters 49–54 emphasizes feminine roles to describe God's relationship to Zion. The interpretive history of DI has been expanded with the awareness of significant images and metaphors for women. Previously overlooked ideas are now highlighted and brought to the fore. Interest in feminist and gender issues, especially in the BOI, has grown within recent years. Hanne Løland in her book on gendered God language in the Bible reads three texts in DI that compare God to a woman and emphasize the bodily connections between mother and child. In 42:14, God is portrayed as a pregnant women giving birth to her child. In 46:3–4, God has carried Israel from pregnancy through birth through to old age. Last, the comparison intensifies in 49:15. God asks (rhetorically) whether a mother can forget her nursing child or have no compassion for the child of her womb. Here YHWH is compared to a mother who loves her child. Some scholars are uneasy with the idea that God would be portrayed in feminine imagery and protest that God's love is contrasted to or greater than that of a mother. However, the same protest could be raised in comparing God with a warrior, or father, or some other masculine figure.

The Text in Contemporary Discussion

One of the most important features of DI's emphasis on Jerusalem/Zion in recent scholarship is the recognition of the importance of feminine figures. The difficulty and beauty of moving into postmodernity is that there is not just one correct interpretation of a given text. The nature and identity of communities that read texts influences how and why interpretations vary. One rabbi explains it this way, asking, "How do donkeys read the Bible?" The answer is: they look for stories about donkeys. When reading a text, everyone brings personal experiences to their interpretation of that text. When women began studying the Bible in seminaries and universities, they brought new questions, ideas, and insights to the fore. Studies of Zion/Jerusalem in Isaiah 40–66 have increased in recent years as scholars, both women and men, incorporate the identity and role of Zion into their reading of the BOI.

Nations

The Text in Its Ancient Context

The term "nations" (Heb., *goyim*) appears throughout Isaiah 40–55; it is a synonym for "coastlands" and "peoples." These chapters contain several descriptions of who or what the nations are and why they are significant in DI. Richard Clifford calls chapter 49 "a press release to all the nations" (Clifford, 150). The coastlands are addressed by the servant who functions as a "light to the nations" (49:1–6). Zion/Israel, once called the slave of rulers, changes places with the nations. The message to the nations is that their rulers will work as ignominious servants, prostrating themselves and licking the dust of the feet of Zion and her children (49:22–23). The oppressors become the oppressed. A technique frequently used in DI called *inner-biblical allusion* is the citation of another biblical text to enhance meaning. The image of Zion's oppressive rulers losing their power is a foil to a text in Jer. 13:18, which portrays the opposite situation: Israel's king and queen mother lose their crowns and must take a lowly seat when Babylon destroys Judah (Willey, 203). In Isaiah 49, the tables are turned. A somewhat different view of the role of the nations is also alluded to in this section. For example, the "coastlands" wait for God and hope in God's powerful arm (51:5). In 52:10b, all nations and "the ends of the earth shall see / the salvation of our God."

The Text in the Interpretive Tradition

An important aspect of biblical studies is textual criticism. Since there are many ancient manuscripts of the Bible in various languages, text critics study these texts to arrive at an authoritative reading of a given word or words when more than one possible reading exists. For Isaiah scholars, the discovery of the Isaiah manuscript among the Dead Sea

Scrolls has given much insight into the BOI. With respect to Isa. 52:5, one of the scribes of the Dead Sea Scrolls made a change in the translation of verse 5, as did the Greek translator in the Septuagint. This may reflect ancient concerns about the meaning and/or significance of this verse. Joseph Blenkinsopp observes that attempts at "a coherent reading of 52:1–12 have not been successful" (Blenkinsopp, 340).

The Text in Contemporary Discussion

Past and present interpretations of the role of the nations in DI have vigorously debated the question of whether DI's prophecies were nationalistic or had a universalistic, inclusive view of the nations, including them among the redeemed. When referring to the nations, some Isaiah commentaries have used highly charged theologized perspectives that go far beyond evidence in the text. The term *goyim* has been translated as "heathens," "pagans," or "gentiles." The messenger "who brings good news" in 52:7 is called an "evangelical herald of the Gospel" in a recent Christian commentary (Lessing, 9). Yet other Christian interpreters see these texts as encouraging missionary work to convert pagans. However, the contemporary concept of conversion is not a feature of Old or New Testament religion (see "Conversion," in Anchor Bible Dictionary, Vol. 1, pp. 1131–33).

The Servant

The Text in Its Ancient Context

The identity and role of the servant in DI is one of the most controversial issues in the BOI.

Reading the servant passages in the context of the Babylonian exile and its aftermath is essential to understanding the servant's role.

Questions asked about the servant abound: Who is the servant? Is the servant an individual, or are there many? Can the servant be identified with any individual important in Israelite history? Is it a collective term applied to all Israel? What is the role or work of the servant? Is the servant a prophet, teacher, priest, or the author of Isaiah 40–55? What is the reason for the servant's suffering?

In 49:1–53:12, the servant appears three times. In 49:1–7, he is called from birth by God to restore the survivors of Israel but laments that his work has been in vain. In 50:4–10, his role is to teach and sustain the weary community. However, he is not well received and endures persecution at their hands. The longest section devoted to the servant is Isa. 52:13–53:12. Though 52:13 begins with an announcement that the servant will prosper and be lifted up, this positive view does not continue. The servant's life is a pattern of rejection, misery, and continual violence from birth until his ignominious death. In the end, the righteous servant who intercedes on behalf of the community will see his descendants prosper, and he will be numbered among the great ones.

The role and possible identity of the servant can be more clearly understood within the sociopolitical setting of the exiles' life under Babylonian rule (Gottwald, 499–501). The prophet's ringing praises of Cyrus the Persian as liberator of the exiles (44:28–45:4) could be seen as threats to the Babylonian Empire. Some among the exiles supported the prophet's view; others feared that his words would bring retaliation against the exiles for their antigovernment stance. Alternately, a pro-Babylon position among the exiles is not hard to imagine. After living there for years, many adapted to this new life, perhaps supporting the status quo of Babylonian rule and their own social and political security. The execution of a traitor can be seen as an understandable response by the Babylonian government (Ceresko, 1–14).

The Text in the Interpretive Tradition

The identity and role of the servant is one of the most discussed issues in DI scholarship. In the late 1800s, Bernhard Duhm proposed that four sections in DI—42:1–4 or 7; 49:1–4; 50:4–9; and 52:13–53:12—were so different in composition, style, and content that they must have come from another author and were inserted into the BOI at a later time. A distinction was made between Israel/Jacob as servant and the innocent servant in these four passages, which came to be called the Suffering Servant Songs. Most scholars today consider the so-called Servant Songs consistent with the literary style and content of the rest of DI. Other occurrences of the term "servant" elsewhere in DI refer to Israel and allude to the suffering of the exiles. The sociopolitical explanations of Norman Gottwald and Anthony Ceresko relating to the servant in Isaiah 52–53 are understandable within the Babylonian context before the return to Judah. They may also shed light on the continuing challenges for community life after the return as described in Isaiah 56–66.

The Text in Contemporary Discussion

Many Christian interpreters identify the "Suffering Servant" exclusively with Jesus and identify those who attacked the servant with Jews. Two problems arise with these views. To speak of Jesus, who lived in the first century CE, would be meaningless to exiles living in Babylonia in the sixth century BCE. In addition, this view fans the fires of antisemitism for those who hold such a misinterpretation today.

Contemporary interpretations of the Suffering Servant have been meaningful to indigenous people in countries around the world. Jorge Pixley (95–96) relates accounts of Latinas in San Salvador and Nicaragua who worked in communities to change their impoverished conditions. Offering educational opportunities and organizing groups of women resulted in the slaying of those who encouraged social action. Pixley compares the deaths of such leaders to that of the servant in Isaiah, calling them martyrs. Attempts at social transformation can and do result in persecution if the government feels threatened.

Another comparison is made between the Suffering Servant and the *minjung* of Korea. This term refers to people who are politically oppressed, economically exploited, socially alienated, religiously discriminated against, and denied education (Moon, 113). In Kwangju, capital of the poorest region in the country, protesters in 1980 demonstrated against the government, which had ignored their plight for years.

Peaceful rallies were put down by military paratroopers, and in the end more than three thousand people were killed or injured. Moon compares the Suffering Servant to the *minjung* who gave their lives to liberate others.

Isaiah 54:1–17

Zion Transformed from Barren Woman and Destroyed City to Mother of Many and Rebuilt City

The Text in Its Ancient Context

The addressee and subject of God's messages in previous chapters is Zion (Isa. 49:14–50:2, 51:2–3; 51:11–52:9). She is described as a barren woman; bride; mother; widow; divorced woman; an afraid and abandoned woman grieving the loss of her children; one who suffered devastation and destruction, famine and sword and captivity; and a destroyed and soon to be rebuilt city. In six verses (54:1–6), the prophet lists all the previously used epithets of the defeated people and then overturns them.

A tent that will be enlarged for all of Zion's children is a metaphor for the expansion of her descendants throughout the world. The dispossessed will now advance to possess and populate the nations (54:3). The shame of abandonment, widowhood, or divorce will be forgotten because God "your Maker is your husband . . . your Redeemer" (54:5).

One of the most striking declarations in this section is God's admission that

> *for a brief moment I abandoned you . . .*
> *in overflowing wrath for a moment*
> *I hid my face from you. (54:7–8)*

Her husband acknowledges her terrible suffering and unjust punishments and promises to amend his ways. In terms of the marriage metaphor, it is understandable that one or both parties might admit their shortcomings. While it is not typical to hear God acknowledge fault in this or any relationship in the Bible, this sentiment was earlier expressed in Isa. 40:2 with God's admission that Jerusalem's penalty was excessive.

Another view of Zion in 54:11–17 is as a city about to be rebuilt. A new Jerusalem is described in fantastical terminology. The image of a bejeweled city recalls descriptions of Mesopotamian palaces (Paul, 427). Jerusalem's children will be taught by God and will live in great prosperity. The city will never be taken over by oppressors; no weapons will be strong enough to overtake it. No one will be able to speak against her.

The Text in the Interpretive Tradition

Does God apologize to Zion for having abandoned her, or is God's wrath against the people justified? Two commentators on Isaiah 40–66 explain God's treatment of Zion in verses 6–7. Instead of "a brief moment," Paul translates "in a fit of rage," reading the Hebrew term *regaʿ* as an "antonym of love," not a measure of time. He further explains that the "Lord's rapprochement with Israel is based not on their regret but on His love" (Paul, 423). Blenkinsopp reads God's statement as a standard accusation used in Assyrian treaties as the result of breaking a treaty (Blenkinsopp, 363). It seems jarring or out of place amid the effusive language of joy to introduce such explanations or defenses of God in these passionate reassurances to Zion.

The Text in Contemporary Discussion

One of the most basic discussions in the Bible, both Old and New Testament, relates to the questions of God's anger and why throughout history innocent people have suffered. The way scholars have interpreted Isa. 54:7–8 serves as an example of the wide range of explanations. Some consider that God's wrath is justified; people deserve punishment for their sinful acts. Others emphasize that a relationship between God and people is based not on strict rules or punitive treatment, but on a familial model that emphasizes love, acceptance, understanding, and forgiveness.

Isaiah 55:1–13

God's Word Is Reliable

The Text in Its Ancient Context

This short chapter is a dense and complicated review of past motifs and allusions to future themes woven together by the underpinnings of the reliability of God's word. As such, it functions to link Isaiah 40–54 to 56–66. The entire BOI is connected by the assertion in 1:20, repeated in 40:5 and 58:14, that "The mouth of YHWH has spoken."

The word that goes forth from God's mouth will accomplish God's purpose for the exiles. Several images are used throughout 55:1–13 to illustrate their future. They will be given the basic sustenance of water and bread and also lavished with wine, milk, and rich food. Offers of such fare to people living in disadvantaged conditions would catch the audience's attention. God's word is compared to rain and snow falling from the heavens; just as these water the earth providing seeds for the sower and bread for the eater, God's word will provide life for the people. Similar images of renewed fertility continue in 55:12–13. A once thorny, weed-filled wilderness will be replaced by the growth of fragrant trees. Those who suffered as they were led into captivity through a hostile desert environment will return to fruitful land and an everlasting memorial that will never be "cut off." The transformation of the wilderness announced numerous times in DI will become a reality.

Another image of transformation, in 55:3–4, recalls God's covenant with David. In a radical change to the original terms of this agreement—that there would always be a Davidic descendant on the throne in Jerusalem—God alters the promise and makes an eternal covenant with the exiles, who will return to Jerusalem. The Davidic monarchy is not mentioned elsewhere in DI; it perhaps is inserted here to allude to the importance of the Davidic kingship in First Isaiah.

The Text in the Interpretive Tradition

A problem with God's promise of a permanent Davidic dynasty is that neither the dynasty nor Jerusalem survived. Here is another reason for exiles to doubt God's power and/or will to restore them. How was DI's audience to understand the arcane reference to the new "everlasting covenant" in 55:3? Many commentaries and articles have taken on these cryptic verses. Some reconceptualize the promise, referring to the "democratization" of the Davidic monarchy in which leadership resides in the entire community. Another explanation is that roles filled by individuals in the past will be taken over by a wider circle of people in the future (Clifford, 192).

The Text in Contemporary Discussion

Chapter 55 sums up motifs from previous chapters. It also functions as a connection with the following chapters. In Isaiah 56–66, the issue of leadership in Jerusalem in the postexilic period continues to be problematic. Reference to the "memorial" and "everlasting sign" of the regeneration of the land is considered by some to be a garden or park that memorializes the return home. Others view it as a metaphor for the renewal of creation. Jewish tradition has interpreted the "memorial, / for an everlasting sign" that will never be cut off (55:13) as a reference to the Sabbath. This refers to the importance of keeping the Sabbath in 56:4–7, as well as the promise to the foreigner and eunuch that they will not be cut off from the community in Jerusalem. It does not, however, resolve the underlying issue—the continuing problem of fulfillment of God's promises to the exiles.

Isaiah 56:1–59:21

Problems after the Return—Relationship between the Returnees and Those Who Remained in Judah

The Text in Its Ancient Context

Chapters 56–66 (TI) are set in Yehud (a term for Judah as a Persian province) after the exiles return to begin life in what remained of their ravaged homeland. The returnees, the Diaspora, include those who left Babylonia as well others who were exiled elsewhere after the destruction of Jerusalem. They joined people who remained in the land after 587 and eked out an existence with no infrastructure: no economic security, no food, and no governing bodies.

Chapters 56–66 continue in a literary style similar to that of 40–55. The same themes and motifs appear with variations. Two major sections in TI (Isa. 56:1–59:21 and 63:1–66:24.)reflect the current troubled realities of life in Yehud. Chapters 60–62, however, focus on hopes for the future in a restored Jerusalem and temple.

In this mixed community, disagreements reach a high pitch. Factions argue about who is in charge, what is considered evidence of faith, what rules govern worship, and who is allowed to participate in this new community. One group emphasizes an inclusive viewpoint, accepting participation by all regardless of ethnicity or background. Another is more exclusive in perspective, especially with respect to foreigners and the indigenous populace.

Chapters 56–59 describe bitter conflicts in the newly constituted Yehud. Issues in Isaiah 56 include proper observation of the Sabbath, rules about sacrificial offerings, and the role of foreigners and eunuchs in worship. The latter are assured that if they keep the Sabbath and the covenant they will not be separated from the community. God will gather outcasts because "my house shall be called a house of prayer / for all peoples" (56:7).

Another issue is misuse of authority by leaders. The shepherds and sentinels who are supposed to protect their community are compared to wild animals and dogs with voracious appetites for food and drink (56:9–12). Leaders are referred to as offspring of a sorceress and are accused of slaughtering their children (57:3–5). Their adulterous mother, the sorceress, is the focus of the attack in 57:6–13. Her sexual behavior is explicitly described in what can be called the most violent, lurid polemic in the Bible. Imagery relating to adultery committed by a woman is found in other prophetic literature. In the book of Hosea, the prophet's wife Gomer is accused of being unfaithful. However, it is not found elsewhere in Isaiah 40–66.

Chapters 58–59 return to the theme of the divided community and inadequate ritual behaviors. The issue in 58:1–9 is the efficacy of fasting. People protest that, while they fast and humble themselves, God does not acknowledge their acts. However, their behaviors belie the significance of fasting: they oppress their workers, quarrel with one another, and engage in acts of violence. An air of sarcasm and impatience underlies God's accusations that they fast only for show. God redefines fasting as acts of social justice: freeing the oppressed; sharing food with the hungry, homes with the homeless, clothes with the naked; and satisfying needs of the afflicted (58:6–7, 10). The grievous nature of the people's offenses intensifies in 59:1–4. Their hands are filled with blood, and they speak lying words; they have corrupted the court system. God's defense is that their own sins prevent them from seeing God's face and hearing God's word.

Chapters 58–59 have a homiletic tone. People claiming to seek God's presence indulge in unacceptable behaviors. If they change these behaviors, they will dwell in the light of God's presence. Conditions that guarantee God's guidance and sustenance are laid out in 58:10–14. People respond with a lament in which they admit their sins and take responsibility for the divisions within the community (59:9–15). In fact, their offenses have contributed to the continuing chaotic conditions.

God grows increasingly indignant at their vile behavior and asks: "Shall I be appeased for these things?" (57:6); "Have I not kept silent and closed my eyes and so you did not fear me?" (57:11); and "Do you call this a fast, a day acceptable to the Lord?" (58:5). Specific references to God's wrath continue in 57:16–17. A finale to all this bloodshed and violence is a spectacular theophany of God as an angry warrior (59:15a–19). God, appalled at the lack of justice, puts on garments of vengeance and a mantle of fury. God's wrath will punish all adversaries and enemies; they will be repaid according to their deeds.

The Text in the Interpretive Tradition

The eunuch laments that he has no children to carry on his name (56:5). But God promises that, if he observes the covenant, he will not be forgotten, and will be given an everlasting "monument and a name" (Heb., *yād vāshēm*). Yad Vashem is the name of a holocaust memorial complex in Jerusalem that preserves the memory of the six million people killed during World War II. Names, photos, films, and other artifacts of those killed ensure that they will have an "everlasting name that will not be cut off."

The Text in Contemporary Discussion

The BOI begins with a blistering critique of people who bring sacrifices and burnt offerings while oppressing the poor in their community (Isa. 1:10–20). God refuses to acknowledge their prayers and warns that they will be devoured by the sword unless they defend the *widow and the orphan*. This phrase is used throughout the Bible; it refers to the neediest in society, who have no means of supporting themselves. Isaiah 58:13 repeats the accusation from Isa. 1:12 that people are "trampling the Sabbath," and redefines the meaning of fasting and Sabbath observation as restoring justice, freeing the oppressed, feeding the hungry, sheltering the homeless, and clothing the naked.

Of all the passages in the Bible cited as a command to the faithful, the one most often repeated is the command to care for the widow and the orphan. Unfortunately, all too many well-intentioned believers direct their attention to other offenses. As a result, the oppressed and needy continue to be ignored, not seen or heard. Society often overlooks the existence of the poor. Data from the National Coalition for the Homeless shows 3.5 million people (1.35 million of them children) experience homelessness in a given year (DeYoung et al., 875).

Isaiah 60:1–62:12

Restoration of Jerusalem and Its Inhabitants

The Text in Its Ancient Context

An issue continuing throughout Isaiah 40–66 is the deferment of God's promise of comfort and deliverance. From the very beginning (Isaiah 40), the disconsolate exiles protested that their

> *way is hidden from the* L*ORD*,
> *and [their] right is disregarded by [their] God.* (40:17)

When the exiles returned to their homeland, hopes of a new and improved life failed to materialize. Life in a fractured and fractious community as described in Isaiah 56–59 brought different problems.

Chapters 60–62 form a stark contrast to the surrounding sections, 56–59 and 63:1–65:16, which portray difficulties, intrigues, and rancorous disagreements among groups in Yehud. From beginning to end, chapters 60–62 emphasize the glorious future of the once devastated Jerusalem. It will be restored to include Zion's children, and also kings and peoples of other nations. Numerous images describe the return of fertility to land and people, the radiance of rebuilt Jerusalem, and the shining beauty of the city and its inhabitants, all of which demonstrate the reversal of Zion's fortune.

One of the most notable features of 60–62 is the reappearance of feminine images of Zion. These include the feminine forms of address, as well as references to Zion as a wife, bride, and mother, as in 49, 52, and 54. Chapter 60 swarms with feminine grammatical forms. Recalling 49:15–21, Zion is again directly addressed by God in 60:1–22 (Wells, 198–202). A key image of the city's restoration in chapter 60 is that of light. Zion will be radiant as nations are drawn to her. God's everlasting glory will replace the light of sun and moon. Also repeated from DI is God's apology (60:10). Because people received a double portion of shame, they will now possess a double portion of everlasting joy (61:7).

Much of Isaiah 60–62 uses motifs and language from 40–55, often showing how the situation of Zion/Jerusalem is renewed and transformed. The people begin a new life in Yehud with a mixed group that includes returnees, those who had stayed in the remains of a destroyed Jerusalem, as well as foreigners with no national or ethnic connections to the original Jacob/Israel community.

The Text in the Interpretive Tradition

The relationship of the nations/foreigners to the returnees is introduced in two ways. Striking images describe the reversal of status among foreigners, kings, nations, and the renewed Zion. Foreigners will build the city walls; kings will bow down to Zion and bring their wealth to her (60:10–12). They will also do the work of shepherding and farming while the once oppressed will serve as priests and ministers of God (61:5–6). Are foreigners accepted or rejected in this new community? One view is that 60:2–7 portrays a tolerance, even acceptance, of gentiles whose offerings God regards as "acceptable on my altar" (Smith-Christopher, 126–27). Reading the same verses, another view is that in Isaiah 60–63, foreigners are viewed in a negative light because of their ancestry, ethnicity, and/or national identity. One explanation for these differing views is that in a later period a *redactor* (editor) of TI acknowledged that foreigners were eventually incorporated into the community.

The Text in Contemporary Discussion

It could be said that cognitive dissonance is a consistent feature of the audiences' mind-set throughout Isaiah 40–66. They hold in tension a belief in God's promise of comfort and extravagant prosperity alongside an experience of continuously deferred hope. Some interpreters have characterized views of the future in TI as *eschatological* or *apocalyptic*. The term *eschatology* refers to an end time or climax of history. The term *apocalyptic* is applied to types of literature that arose in the Hellenistic and Roman period around 333 BCE, several centuries after the destruction of Babylon. Works such as the books of *Enoch* and Daniel anticipated catastrophic and imminent upheavals: earthquakes, massacres, world war against unholy nations, and the like. Referring to DI or TI as eschatological or apocalyptic is misleading and vague. When people in any age imagine a better future in positive and exaggerated terms, it does not necessarily indicate that they are thinking of the end time, or the last days. It can be a sign of hope for what is to come.

Isaiah 63:1–66:24

The People Lament God's Unfulfilled Promises and Community Divisions Continue

The Text in Its Ancient Context

Chapters 60–62 describe the restoration of Jerusalem and its inhabitants. Jerusalem's radiant light replaces sun and moon. Daughter Zion's fortunes are reversed. Violence ceases. Absent from this idyllic picture is any note of the bitter divisions among the community that marked chapters 56–59. The last chapters of the BOI (63–66) return to the somber view of the state of affairs in Yehud with an additional feature. A contrast is drawn between the fates of two groups within the community. Those engaging in illegitimate ritual practices are "destined to the sword," while God's servants will rejoice in Jerusalem.

Chapter 63 begins with the appearance of a mysterious figure whose garments are splattered with the blood of Edom. God is portrayed here as a warrior who has taken vengeance against Edom, a longtime enemy of Israel. A number of commentators, offended by the violent image, deny that the wrathful warrior could be God. However, the motif of God's wrath throughout Isaiah 57–59, and the warrior image elsewhere in TI (in 59:15b–19 and 66:14b–16), are consistent with God as an angry warrior. A major difference between these passages is that in chapter 59 God's anger is directed against injustices within the Jerusalem community; in chapter 63, it is aimed at Israel's enemies.

The remaining chapters consist of a lament in which people bemoan the loss of God's help (63:7–64:12), and God's response to their desperate pleas (65:1–15). Jerusalem's destiny is portrayed in chapter 66 in surprising and graphic images of reward for the faithful and punishment for the intransigent reprobates.

In the lament, people again remind God of unfulfilled promises. The tone of their complaints reaches a desperate pitch. They ask:

Where is the one who led Moses through the sea? Where is your zeal and your might, your compassion? They blame God for hardening their hearts and causing them to sin. Still suffering from the loss of their nation and their temple, they ask, "Will you keep silent, and punish us so severely?" (64:12). God speaks in self-defense, asserting that though "I held out my hands all day long" (65:2), rebellious people angered God with idolatrous rituals. God warns them that they will receive full payment for their actions and promises to destine them to slaughter (65:1–15).

Not all will be destroyed in the fiery blast of God's anger. A group within the community, the servants who did not forsake God, will inherit blessings. The contrasting destinies of these two groups are listed in 65:13–15. The chosen, God's servants who have followed God's commands, will live and rejoice in a glorious new Jerusalem. God is about to create a new heaven and earth where all ills will be forgotten. Descriptive language for this new state of life in chapter 65 is taken from earlier Isaiah texts, including the peaceable community, where predatory animals and their prey will eat together (11:6–9), and from the blossoming wilderness of Isaiah 35.

The last chapter alludes to previous motifs from chapters 60–62. One of the most striking is the recurrence of Jerusalem as a mother and wife. In 66:7–13, Zion/Jerusalem is portrayed as a woman giving birth after a speedy labor, nursing the child from her glorious bosom, carrying the baby in her arms, and dandling the baby on her knees. God is also compared to a mother and to a midwife who assists in the delivery of the child. These images emphasize physical features of a mother giving birth and caring for her child. Her birth pains last for only a moment. Her womb is opened: 66:9 literally translated is "breaking" (the membrane). She nurses the child from her "consoling breast" and "glorious nipple" (Franke 2009).

These images are complicated. Zion/Jerusalem and God are portrayed as mother. In previous chapters, these same images appear in similar combinations. God is a woman gasping in labor pains

(42:13–14); God is compared to both a father and to a mother in labor (45:10), and to a nursing mother who has compassion for the child of her womb (49:5). Some scholars disagree that God is portrayed here or anywhere as a woman and read these passages as a contrast, saying that God's love is greater than that of a mother. It is difficult to defend such a position in view of the passages cited above. Images of Zion as a bride, a once barren woman, a mother who has lost her children, a woman once captive now dressed in beautiful garments, a widow, a divorced woman, a wife rejected and then taken back by God are recapitulated in glowing portrayals of God and Jerusalem/Zion in Isaiah 60–62 and 65–66.

The BOI contains a pastiche of ideas and forms. Ritual offenses are contrasted with emphasis on appropriate offerings and Sabbath observance. Many nations will be called to Jerusalem to bring offerings to God on Mount Zion. The last verse, 66:24, describes a ghastly scene: the bodies of all who have rebelled against God burn in unquenchable fire. However, in Jewish tradition, books of the Bible should end with a positive perspective. Therefore, verse 24 is sometimes followed by the repetition of verse 23:

From new moon to new moon,
And from Sabbath to Sabbath,
All flesh shall come to worship before me
All flesh will come to worship before God.

The Text in the Interpretive Tradition

While the violence of the Divine Warrior image is shocking, it has been used from New Testament times to the present. The bloodied warrior appears in Revelation 14, describing the fall of Babylon. The son of man and others wield sharp sickles, harvesting the earth of evil. The "wine press of God's wrath" yields vast quantities of blood. It has also been used to illustrate and justify war in US history in the name of truth and justice. The Divine Warrior inspired Julia Ward Howe to compose a Civil War song still sung today in many contexts. Recall the first verse of this song.

> *Mine eyes have seen the glory of the coming of the Lord,*
> *He is trampling out the vintage where the grapes of wrath are stored,*
> *He hath loosed the fateful lightning of his terrible swift sword;*
> *His truth is marching on. Glory, Glory, Halleluiah.*

Another use of Isaiah 66 is found in Brahms's *Eine Deutsches Requiem*. Grieving mourners long for the one who has died, but they are reassured: "I will again behold you, and your heart will be joyful. . . . Look at me. . . . I have found comfort at last. I will give you comfort, as one whom his own mother comforts."

Selections from the BOI have caused difficulties for some Roman Catholic authorities that have recently made changes in the liturgy. The document *Liturgiam Authenticum* aims at using transcendent language and warns against Isaiah texts because they often portray God as too human. However, use of images taken from human life and experience in the BOI is what makes it such an important text in Judeo-Christian tradition. The Bible is *the primary* source of "sacred vocabulary." Problematic texts should be used, explored, read, and discussed. Texts that make a divine-human connection and cause problems for readers are precisely those texts that advance the development of theological and religious thinking.

The Text in Contemporary Discussion

After the destruction of the Twin Towers on 9/11, the world was forever changed. Scholars responded to this event, realizing the need to address directly questions of vengeance and violence in the Bible, both Old and New Testaments. At the annual meeting of the Society of Biblical Literature that followed 9/11, many research and study groups changed their direction and began to focus on these issues in the Bible, in religion, in churches, and in other religious bodies. This topic now forms a major body of study in areas of scholarship (Franke and O'Brien). Religious groups—Jews, Christians, and Muslims—also make this issue part of interfaith discussions.

WORKS CITED

Anderson, Gary A. 1991. *A Time to Mourn, a Time to Dance: The Expression of Grief and Joy in Israelite Religion*. University Park: Pennsylvania State University Press.

Berges, Ulrich. 2010. "Farewell to Deutero-Isaiah or Prophecy without a Prophet." In *Congress Volume Ljubljana 2007*, edited by André Lemaire, 575–95. VTSup 133. Leiden: Brill.

Blenkinsopp, Joseph. 2002. *Isaiah 40–55*. AB. New York: Doubleday.

Brueggemann, Walter. 1998. *Isaiah 40–66*. Westminster Bible Commentary. Louisville: Westminster John Knox.

Ceresko, Anthony R. 2002. *Prophets and Proverbs: More Studies in Old Testament Poetry and Biblical Religion*. Quezon City, Philippines: Claretian.

Clifford, Richard J. 1984. *Fair Spoken and Persuading: An Interpretation of Second Isaiah*. New York: Paulist.

Davies, Andrew. 2007. "Oratorio as Exegesis: The Use of the Book of Isaiah in Handel's *Messiah*." *BibInt* 15:464–84.

DeYoung, Curtiss Paul, Wilda C. Gafney, Leticia Guardiola-Saenz, George E. Tinker, and Frank M. Yamada, eds. 2009. *The Peoples' Bible*. Minneapolis: Fortress Press.

Franke, Chris A. 1991. "The Function of the Satiric Lament over Babylon in Second Isaiah (xlvii)." *VT* 41:408–18.

Franke, Chris A. 1994. *Isaiah 46, 47, and 48: A New Literary-Critical Reading*. Biblical and Judaic Studies 3. Winona Lake, IN.: Eisenbrauns.

Franke, Chris A. 2009. "'Like a Mother I Have Comforted You:' The Function of Figurative Language in Isaiah 1:7–26 and 66:7–14." In *The Desert Will Bloom: Poetic Visions in Isaiah, Ancient Israel and Its Literature*, edited by A. Joseph Everson and Hyun Chul Paul Kim, 35–55. Atlanta: Society of Biblical Literature.

Franke, Chris, and Julia M. O'Brien, eds. 2010. *Aesthetics of Violence in the Prophets*. New York: T&T Clark.

Gottwald, Norman K. 1985. *The Hebrew Bible: A Socio-Literary Introduction*. Philadelphia: Fortress Press.

Isasi-Díaz, Ada María. 1995. "By the Rivers of Babylon: Exile as a Way of Life." In *Reading from This Place*. Vol. 1, *Social Location and Biblical Interpretation in the United States*, edited by Fernando F. Segovia and Mary Ann Tolbert, 149–63. Minneapolis: Fortress Press.

Kim, Hyun Chul Paul. 2009. "The Spider Poet: Signs and Symbols in Isaiah 41." In *The Desert Will Bloom: Poetic Visions in Isaiah*, edited by A. Joseph Everson and Hyun Chul Paul Kim, 159–80. SBLAIL. Atlanta: Society of Biblical Literature.

Kruger, Paul A. 1997. "The Slave Status of the Virgin Daughter Babylon in Isaiah 47:2: A Perspective from Anthropology." *JNSL* 23:143–51.

Lack, Rémi. 1973. *La symbolique de livre d'Isaïe: Essaie sur l'image littéraire comme élément de structuration*. AnBib. Rome: Pontifical Biblical Institute.

Lessing, R. Reed. 2011. *Isaiah 40–55: A Theological Exposition of Sacred Scripture*. St Louis: Concordia.

Løland, Hanne. 2008. *Silent or Salient Gender? The Interpretation of Gendered God-Language in the Hebrew Bible, Exemplified in Isaiah 42, 46 and 49*. Tübingen: Mohr Siebeck.

Lund, Øystein. 2007. *Way Metaphors and Way Topics in Isaiah 40–55*. FAT. Tübingen: Mohr Siebeck.

Moon, Cyris Heesuk. 1999. "Isaiah 52:13–53:12: An Asian Perspective." In *Return to Babel: Global Perspectives on the Bible*, edited by John R. Levison and Priscilla Pope-Levison, 107–13. Louisville: Westminster John Knox.

Moore, Megan Bishop, and Brad E. Kelle. 2011. *Biblical History and Israel's Past: The Changing Study of the Bible and History*. Grand Rapids: Eerdmans.

Muilenburg, James. 1956. "The Book of Isaiah: Chapters 40–66." In *Interpreter's Bible*. Vol. 5, *Ecclesiastes, the Song of Songs, Isaiah, Jeremiah*, edited by George A. Buttrick, 381–773. New York: Abingdon.

Newsom, Carol A., Sharon H. Ringe, and Jacqueline E. Lapsley, eds. 2012. *Women's Bible Commentary*. 3rd ed. Louisville: Westminster John Knox.

Paul, Shalom M. 2012. *Isaiah 40–66: Translation and Commentary*. Eerdmans Critical Commentary. Grand Rapids: Eerdmans.

Pixley, Jorge. 1999. "Isaiah 52:13–53:12: A Latin American Perspective." In *Return to Babel: Global perspectives on the Bible*, edited by John R. Levison and Priscilla Pope-Levison, 95–100. Louisville: Westminster John Knox.

Schökel, Luis Alonso. 1987. "Isaiah." In *The Literary Guide to the Bible*, edited by Robert Alter and Frank Kermode, 165–84. Cambridge, MA: Belknap Press of Harvard University Press.

Smith, Mark. 1990. *The Early History of God: Yahweh and the Other Deities in Ancient Israel*. San Francisco: Harper & Row.

Smith, Mark. 2001. *The Origins of Biblical Monotheism: Israel's Polytheistic Background and the Ugaritic Texts*. Oxford: Oxford University Press.

Smith-Christopher, Daniel L. 2002. *A Biblical Theology of Exile*. Minneapolis: Fortress Press.

Soares-Prabhu, George M. 1995. "Laughing at Idols: The Dark Side of Biblical Monotheism (an Indian Reading of Isaiah 44:9–20." In *Reading from This Place*. Vol. 1, *Social Location and Biblical Interpretation in the United States*, edited by Fernando F. Segovia and Mary Ann Tolbert, 149–63. Minneapolis: Fortress Press.

Tiemeyer, Lena-Soria. 2011. *For the Comfort of Zion: The Geographical and Theological Location of Isaiah 40–55*. Leiden: Brill.

Torrey, Charles Cutler. 1928. *The Second Isaiah: A New Interpretation*. Edinburgh: T&T Clark.

Tull, Patricia K. 2009. "Persistent Vegetative States: People and Plants and Plants as People in Isaiah." In *The Desert Will Bloom: Poetic Visions in Isaiah*, edited by A. Joseph Everson and Hyun Chul Paul Kim, 17–35. SBLAIL. Atlanta: Society of Biblical Literature.

Wells, Roy D. 2009. "'They All Gather, They Come to You': History, Utopia, and the Reading of Isaiah 49:18–16 and 60:4–16." In *The Desert Will Bloom: Poetic Visions in Isaiah*, edited by A. Joseph Everson and Hyun Chul Paul Kim, 187–216. SBLAIL. Atlanta: Society of Biblical Literature.

Willey, Patricia Tull. 1997. *Remember the Former Things: The Recollection of Previous Texts in Second Isaiah*. SBLDS. Atlanta: Scholars Press.